The Human & Environmental cost of Wars

The Human & Environmental cost of Wars

The Human & Environmental cost of Wars

The Human & Environmental cost of Wars

Abdul Rahman S. Magba-Kamara

The Human & Environmental cost of Wars

The Human & Environmental cost of Wars

DEDICATION

This book is dedicated to my late mother in-law Mrs. Isabel Logan (RIP) the kindest and sweetest mother, grandma, and mother in-law in the whole wide world. you will always be in our prayers. To John Logan my father in-law, a sweet and compassionate man I have ever known. Jane Kamara, a sweet and loving mother to our children. To Seuti Abdul Rahman., Abdul Rahman Jr., Princess Isabella, Abdul Aziz and Abdul Latif.. To all the brave men and women in our Armed Forces for their dedication to make our nation safe, and to those who served our nation gallantly during the Bosnia conflict the Persian Gulf and the Middle-East and to the families of all the brave men and women in the armed forces, who had to powerlessly watch their loved ones suffer from the ill effects of exposure to depleted uranium and to all the civilians who were directly or indirectly affected by such exposures.

The Human & Environmental cost of Wars

TABLE OF CONTENTS

LISTS OF TABLE

The Human & Environmental cost of Wars
LIST OF ABBREVATIONS

AACR	American Association for Cancer Research
ARDEC	Armament Research, Development and Engineering Center
BNFL	British Nuclear Fuels
COGEMA	Compagnie generale des matieres nucleaires
DU	Depleted Uranium
DCFS	Dose Conversion Factors
DOE	Department of Energy
EEA	European Environmental Agency
EMRTC	Energetic Materials Research Technology
EPA	Environmental Protection Agency (USA)
FAO	Food and Agricultural Organization (United Nations)
FAEA	Federal Atomic Energy Agency
GAO	General Accounting Office
GWRI	Gulf War Related Illnesses
IAEA	International Atomic Energy Agency
IMR	Institute of Medical Report
JNFL	Japan Nuclear Fuel Limited
KAERI	Korean Atomic Energy Research Institute
KEPEHC	Kinetic Energy Penetrator Environmental and Health Considerations

The Human & Environmental cost of Wars

NATO	North Atlantic Treaty Organization
NEA	Nuclear Energy Agency
NECSA	Nuclear Energy Corporation of South Africa
NGWRC	National Gulf War Resource Center
NMMT	New Mexico Institute of Mining and Technology
NSAID	National Security and International Affairs Division
OECD	Organization for Economic Co-operation and Development
PAC	Presidential Advisory Committee
PNNL	Pacific Northwest National Laboratory
RDD	Radiation Dispersing Devices
RS	Royal Society
RPGVI	Research on Persian Gulf Veterans Illness
SVAC	Senate Veterans Affairs' Committee
TERA	Terminal Effects Research and Analysis
TMI	Three Mile Island
UMRC	Uranium Medical Research Center
URENCO	British Dutch German Consortium (Uranium Enrichment Consortium)
USACHPPM	U. S. Army Center for Health Promotion and Preventive Medicine
USSR	Union of Soviet Socialist Republic
USACS	United States Army Chemical School
USDOD	United States Department of Defense
USNRC	United States Nuclear Regulatory Commission

The Human & Environmental cost of Wars

USVA   United States Veterans Administration

SIT   Swiss Institute of Technology

The Human & Environmental cost of Wars

PREFACE

The human and environmental cost of wars is presented with a particular focus on the use of munitions containing depleted uranium during military conflicts. Depleted Uranium (DU), a low-level radioactive waste of isotopic enrichment uranium, has been identified as a definitive contaminant on battlefields in the Balkans, the Middle-East, and the Persian Gulf. The use of armor-piercing ammunitions made from depleted uranium by the USSR (Soviet Union) in the Afghanistan war, the use of munitions containing depleted uranium by the North Atlantic Treaty Organization (NATO) troops in the Balkans, and the two Gulf Wars, for example, has raised concerns among members of the international community about depleted uranium exposure among military personnel and civilian populations.

This book is about the long-term cost of wars on human health and the environment, the health risks factors to humans and communities and environmental hazards of the long-term detrimental consequences of the use of weapons containing depleted uranium in military conflicts. It includes a review of methods for the prevention and mitigation of such effects. The book presents methods for effective management and containment strategies of depleted uranium and other technological agents. It supports the development and implementation of community support services to be integrated into mitigation strategies. Mitigation strategies for exposures to depleted uranium and other toxins should involve technological, economic, psychological, and support factors.

The Human & Environmental cost of Wars

CHAPTER 1

INTRODUCTION

Depleted uranium (DU), a low-level radioactive waste of the isotopic enrichment of natural uranium, has been identified as a definitive contaminant in international military conflicts in Bosnia, Kosovo and the Persian Gulf. Its etiological role in the genesis of Gulf War disease has been the subject of sustained controversy since the end of the first Gulf War. Numerous scientific and epidemiological studies have shown evidence of both chemical and radiological toxic properties of uranium isotopes in the environment in the Balkans, the Persian Gulf, and the Middle East, and also in the bodies of veterans who were deployed to those areas.

MacDiarmid, Keogh, Hooper, McPhaul, Squibb, Kane, DiPino, Kabat, Kaup, Anderson, Hoover, Brown, Hamilton, Jacobson-Kram, Burrow, and Walsh (2000) studies health effects of depleted uranium on exposed Gulf War veterans. They found the toxic, teratogenic, mutagenic, teratogenic, and carcinogenic effects and increased frequencies of related chromatic exchange in soldiers as a result of depleted uranium exposure. The United States Army Center for Health Promotion and Preventive Medicine Report for Gulf War Related Illnesses suggests that, "the first reported combat use of depleted uranium muni

The Human & Environmental cost of Wars

tions was in the Gulf War in January 1991 in which American and British tanks and aircraft used depleted uranium as armor-piercing penetrators" (USACHPPM 2000, p. 20).

Since then, Marshall, Darvis and Sherbourne (1999) of the National Security Institute noted that a review of the scientific literature as it pertains to Gulf War illnesses has been carried out to assess the health risks associated with the use of depleted uranium munitions. The first study to assess the health risk associated with the use of DU was initiated in the late 1990s by the U.S. Department of Defense (USDOD). Researchers Fetter and Von Hippel (1999) of the Royal Society carried out a fairly comprehensive study of the hazards posed by depleted uranium munitions for United States Department of Defense. To help the military characterize the particulates generated during depleted uranium impacts on armored vehicles, Pacific Northwest National Laboratory (PNNL) researchers, performed extensive depleted uranium weapons testing for the United States Army (Parkhurst, Szrom, Guilmette, Holmes, Cheng, Kenoyer, Collins, Sanders, Fliszar, Gold, Beckman, and Long, 2004). Another study (Marshall, 2005) examined other potential health effects including the effects of radiological dose at the site of embedded fragments and possible chemically induced health effects.

The results of Marshall (2005:14) findings indicate that "claims of significant increases for depleted uranium-exposed veterans and significant increases for their progeny are not supported by study findings." Marshall's findings did not support previous claims of increases in health risks for Iraqi civilians; the health risks for Iraqi civilians were predicted to be very small. Claims of observable increases in Leukemia and birth defects from dep

The Human & Environmental cost of Wars

leted uranium exposure are not supported in Marshall's study. His study reported that the Pacific National Laboratory data were used to predict possible veteran health effects. The conclusions of the Pacific Northwest National Laboratory studies clearly did not support assertions of significant and observable increases in cancers as a result of exposure to depleted uranium munitions. The findings and conclusions of the Pacific National Laboratory depleted uranium studies did not support the findings of Marshall and other scientific and medical studies. For instance, irradiation of 235 uranium on the growth, behavior and some biochemical changes in the brain in neonatal rats in experiment by Gu, Zhu, Wang, and Yang (2001) and earlier findings confirmed earlier findings which show kidneys and bones as the predominant target organs for DU isotopes. Gu et al. (2001) bio-distribution studies also identified the secondary sites as the lymphatic, respiratory, reproductive, and central nervous systems.

Miller's (1986), and Durarakovic's (1999, 2003) studies of undiagnosed illnesses on military personnel and civilians identified the medical effects of internal contamination with uranium, suggesting that exposure to uranium isotopes and radioactive toxins were the cause of their undiagnosed illnesses. Skorga, Persell, Arangie, Gilbert-Palmer, Winters, Stokes, et al. (2003) study basic radio-toxicology and chemical toxicology of uranium isotopes. Little (2002) studied the potential health effects of Radiation Dispersing Devices (RDD) from data based on Japanese bomb survivors, nuclear testing, and laboratory research. The finding in other studies confirms incidents of hapatocellular carcinoma among Japanese atomic bomb survivors (Sharp, Mizuno, Cologne, Fukuhara, Fujiwara, Tokuoka et. al 2003).

The Human & Environmental cost of Wars

These scientific and medical research finding has confirmed what has been clearly determined throughout two decades of research that exposure to radioactive waste of the isotopic enrichment of natural uranium is hazardous to human health and the environment. Furthermore, medical findings from the quantitative analysis of depleted uranium isotopes in British, Canadian and U.S. Gulf War veterans by Horan, Dietz and Durakovic (2002) showed depleted uranium isotopes detection in British, Canadian, and American veterans as long as nine years after inhalation exposure to radioactive dusts.

The use of armor-piercing ammunition made from depleted uranium during con-flicts in the Balkans and the Persian Gulf raised concerns about depleted uranium exposure among military personnel and civilians. In Rostker's (1998, p. 4) environmental report to the United States Department of Defense on Gulf War Related Illnesses, Rostker con-demned the use of radioactive and toxic chemicals in ammunition as

> Heralding a dangerous new era in land warfare, one in which the line between con-ventional and unconventional warfare is seen as irreversibly blurred.

Rostker claimed that by the end of the Persian Gulf Wars, both the United States and the NATO coalition forces had introduced large quantities of armor-piercing ammunition made of depleted uranium contaminated equipment on the battlefields of Kuwait, Southern Iraq and Saudi Arabia.

The Human & Environmental cost of Wars

After Gulf War I, and the subsequent wars in the Balkans, a National Gulf War Resource Center (NGWRC) scientist conducted a study for the presence of high chemical toxicity on veterans who were deployed in those wars. The finding in that toxicity study suggests the presence of high levels of chemical toxicity in veterans who were victims of ammunitions containing depleted uranium from friendly fire (Fahey, 1998). In case-by-case narratives, the NGWRC study linked an increased incidence of cancers, birth defects, and other syndromes in veterans who were exposed to ammunitions coated to depleted uranium. Such studies demonstrated the need for better information from the scientific and medical communities to find ways to mitigate the chemical toxicity of ammunitions coated with depleted uranium.

Such mitigation is essential, particularly for drinking water supplies and agricultural food products. Current understanding of its etiology seems far from adequate. After the U.S. military, along with NATO and Afghan military troops conducted a large operation in Southeast of Zormat in the Shahi-Kot Valley and Arma Mountains in early March 2000 to destroy al Qaeda and Taliban forces in an operation code named Operation Anaconda, teams of medical nuclear physicists, including Miller (1986), Lubenau and Strom (2000) and Durakovic (2003) studied the populations of Islamabad, Spin Gar, Tora Bora, and Kabul. Little (2003) studied the proportion of thyroid cancers associated with background radiation on survivors of in the Japanese atomic bombs. Their reports identified civilians with symptoms similar to those of the Gulf War Syndrome.

Analysis of depleted uranium's hazardous effect on the environment in Afghanistan by Durakovic (2003, p.530-532) and a team of medical nuclear physicists revealed uranium

The Human & Environmental cost of Wars

concentration up to 200 times higher in districts heavily bombarded by U.S. and NATO troops. Their analysis of the soil samples for uranium levels in the bombsites in the districts of Tora Bora, Yaka Toot, Lal Mal, Makam Khan Farm, Arda Farm, Bibi Mahro, Poli Cherki, and the Kabul airport showed values two to three times higher than worldwide concentration levels of 2 to 3 mg/kg, and significantly higher concentration in water than the maximum permissible levels by the World Health Organization.

Durakovic, Dietz and Zimmerman's (2003) uranium environmental exposure analysis study in Afghanistan districts that were heavily bombarded during the war documented the discovery of more than 350 metric tons of depleted uranium deposited in the environment, and 3-6 million grams of depleted uranium aerosol released into the atmosphere. Durakovic and his team of medical and nuclear physicists also conducted an experimental analysis to determine depleted uranium's health exposure factors in civilian populations in areas that were heavily bombarded by the United States and NATO forces during the Afghanistan war. They wanted to determine whether the symptoms they discovered in veterans with Gulf War Syndromes were the same symptoms present in those populations. The team of medical and nuclear physicists collected urine samples from 24 symptomatic subjects. The team divided the study population into two groups: control and experimental subjects.

The control subjects were selected among the symptom-free residents in the non-targeted areas and the experimental groups were selected from districts that were heavily

The Human & Environmental cost of Wars

bombarded during the war. All the samples collected from the 24 experimental subjects were analyzed for the concentration and ratio of four uranium isotopes using multi-collector, inductively coupled plasma ionization and ratio mass spectrometry. The analysis of the findings from Durakovic and his team revealed Uranium concentrations up to 200 times higher in the experimental groups who were bombardment-free.

Cell biology toxicology scholars Arfsten, Still, and Ritchie's (2001) research findings confirmed the toxic effects of uranium on renal cells in reproduction and fetal development. Pellmar, Keyser, Emery and Hogan's (1999) neuro-toxicological study of the brain on rats embedded with depleted uranium confirmed its retention in the sections of the hippocampus, a ridge in the floor of each lateral ventricle of the brain that consists mainly of great matter and has a central role in memory.

In summary, the full impact of fine particles of depleted uranium oxide on human body cannot be fully understood because there is little information on the precise and accurate dose assessment and the dynamics of internalized particles by which cell organ damage occurs. Despite the lack of a precise and accurate dose assessment there is mounting scientific and epidemiological evidence from both animal and in vitro studies that suggest deleterious effects on human health. DU particles from both radiological action and chemical toxicity indicate that uranium weapons are hazardous to human health and the environment.

This book will provide an assessment of the effects of munitions containing depleted uranium on civilians, military personnel and civilian populations. It also focuses on

The Human & Environmental cost of Wars

the environmental hazards caused by the use of such weapons. The organizational structure of this book is divided into six chapters.

Chapter 1 introduces the objective of the study and argues that munitions containing depleted uranium are hazardous to human health and the environment. It discusses the etiological role of depleted uranium exposure in the genesis of Gulf War related illnesses, which has been the subject of sustained controversy since the end of the first Gulf War. This chapter highlights some of the medical and scientific research findings showing the toxic, mutagenic, teratogenic, and carcinogenic human health risks and the environmental hazards as a result of depleted uranium exposure.

Chapter 2 presents the statement of the problem, and the legal and political issues surrounding the use of radioactive waste in military weapons. It describes today's effective conventional anti-tank weapons containing depleted uranium designed to penetrate tank armor in order to kill or disable the tank crews. It will also enumerate some of the dangerous radioactive weapons in the military arsenals of Nations or individual states have contributed to the proliferation of those weapons.

Chapter 3 presents an examination of the relevant literature on depleted uranium toxicity on human health and the environment. It discusses and reviews scientific and medical research on the dangers of the use of munitions containing depleted uranium to human health and the environment.

Chapter 4 describes the methodological approach employed in this exploratory study. Grounded theory is employed to analyze and explain the experience and meaning of

The Human & Environmental cost of Wars

the Gulf War syndrome in the lives of veterans who were deployed in the Gulf War. The method of approach in this study is in the tradition of a disciplined qualitative research method espoused by previous qualitative researchers to help identify themes critical to our understanding the relationships among depleted uranium munitions, human health risks, environmental hazards, and various mitigation strategies. The analytic and thematic approach in this book is typified by simultaneous data generation and analysis, and the use of intensive analytic processes that include constant comparison, levels of coding, and theoretical sampling.

Chapter 5 will discuss themes and categorize the data that emerged from the documentary materials. In the categorization of the data into themes, constant comparative analysis is used to identify statements that support both sides of this controversial issue. Medical and epidemiological journals and print media provided the texts used to identify themes critical to understand the human health risk and environmental hazards of depleted uranium use.

Chapter 6 discusses mitigation procedures from a different disaster management sociological paradigm, a perspective of emergency disaster management to ensure a safer and healthier environment, free from the hazards and dangers of environmental contaminants. In conclusion, the book will suggest policies that the international community should adopt to alleviate threats from radioactive weapons.

CHAPTER 2

STATEMENT OF THE PROBLEM

2.1. Depleted Uranium Use Endangers Human Health and Damages the Environment

Since the end of the First Gulf War, many questions remain about the nature and causes of health problems affecting military personnel deployed in the Persian Gulf region. Medical researchers conducted a series of epidemiological studies since the end of the Gulf War to determine the nature and causes of the health problems. Stretch, Bliese, Marlowe, Wright, Knudson, and Hoover (1995) studied health symtomatolgy of Pennsylvania veterans and service personnel of the Gulf War.

Pierce (1997) conducted research on the physical and emotional health of Gulf War veteran women. Pierce, Antonakos and Deroba (1999) examined health care utilization and satisfaction concerning gender-specific health problems among military women. Gray, Smith, Knoke and Heller (1999) examined the postwar hospitalization experience of Gulf War veterans exposed to chemical munitions destruction at Khamisiyah. Their research focused on the diagnoses of infectious diseases, including mycoplasmic fermentas and four types of viruses.

The Human & Environmental cost of Wars

Fukuda, Nisenbaum, Stewart, Thompson, Robin, Washko, Noah, Barrett, Randall, Herwaldt, Mawle, and Reeves (1998) looked at chronic multi-system illnesses affecting Air force veterans. Gilory (1998) studied Canadian forces personnel involved in the 1991 conflict in the Persian Gulf. Unwin, Blatchley, Coker, et al. (1999) examined the health of United Kingdom servicemen who served in the Persian Gulf War. Gray, Smith, Knoke and Heller (1999) looked at the postwar hospitalization experience of Gulf War veterans possibly exposed to chemical munitions destruction at Khamisiyah, Iraq. A report on the pre - valence of Gulf War Veterans' illnesses was prepared by Lea Steele (2000). Steele's report, which was presented to the Research Advisory Committee (RAC) on Gulf War Veterans' illnesses, identified a complex set of challenges. The set of challenges identified in Steele's report are symptoms and general health status, brain and nervous system functions, the diagnosis for exposure and interactions of exposures to chemical weapons, pyriodostigmine bromide for veterans who were ill as well as for the clinicians, researchers, and government agencies charged with understanding and addressing these conditions.

The first time the American public was informed about the puzzling array of symptoms reported by soldiers who had fought in the Persian Gulf War was in a story published in the *New York Times* (November 22, 1999) by Hilton Jones. Jones reported that undiagnosed symptoms first began in Indiana in early 1992, when soldiers in two reserve units began to experience headaches, rashes and hair loss, and occasionally failed memories. According to Jones' (*New York Times* November 22, 1999, p.A1) article,

> The symptoms, in some of these cases were severe enough to require hospitalization. Over the next year, hundreds and then thousands of veterans began showing up

at hospitals run by the Department of Veterans Affairs with these and a wide array of symptoms

Jones identified a typical sequence of events surrounding veterans' reports on symptoms.

> First there are complaints of severe but undiagnosed symptoms, then the sufferers hear about others experiencing the same symptoms and began to trade information, then there is the naming of a possible new disease, and finally there is a plea for an investigation of the symptom clusters (*New York Times* November 22, 1999, p.A1).

Jones concluded his article by reporting that some of the veterans found that their complaints were dismissed by Veteran Administration doctors as psychosomatic or stress related.

Official reports began to be circulated as early as 2000 about troops' exposure to depleted uranium during the Gulf War. A National Security and International Affairs Division report entitled "Depleted Uranium Health Effects" identified depleted uranium as associated with hazards to human health. It stated, "As a low-level radioactive heavy metal, the potential for health effects are twofold: effects from radiation and effects from chemical toxicity" (NSAID 2000, p. 4).

The NSAID report also mentioned that the United States was not the only country that used munitions containing depleted uranium. It reported that the United Kingdom, Russia, Turkey, Thailand, Israel, Pakistan, and France are also developing weapon systems utilizing depleted uranium. The report cautioned clinical investigators not to misinterpret the results of their observable variance. It cautioned clinical investigators not to combine their observed variances of a small number of veterans with elevated uranium levels with

The Human & Environmental cost of Wars

those veterans who had prior complex medical histories. The report indicates that exposed veterans with embedded fragments of depleted uranium who continue to have elevated uranium levels in their urine in some cases, to lower on computerized tests assessing problem-solving efficiency and to high levels of the prolactin hormone associated with reproductive health.

According to the NSAID report evaluations, in 1997 29 of 51 Gulf War veterans, many of whom have embedded fragments, indicate that, to date, none of these veterans show any evidence of adverse kidney effects associated with exposure to depleted uranium. How -ever, the NSAID report did not rule out the possibility for potential health effects due to exposure from depleted uranium.

A report published in the *Baltimore Sun* (February 4, 2001) claimed that some of the armor-piercing, tanks containing depleted uranium ammunitions used by the U. S. military were contaminated with highly radioactive substances, possibly including plutonium. The report alleged that more than 30 tons of depleted uranium was deposited in Iraq during the Gulf War. Further, it mentioned that researchers at the Swiss Institute of Technology (SIT) discovered that depleted uranium munitions used in Kosovo were contaminated with uranium-236, an isotope of uranium found in natural uranium ore.

In addition to unexplained somatic symptoms, there have been reports of possible increased rates of various medical and psychological illnesses among Gulf War veterans and civilian populations in countries in the Gulf War region. There have also been concerns about the possible increased rates of birth defects among children born after the war to both

The Human & Environmental cost of Wars

male and female Gulf War veterans and civilians in the Gulf War region countries that were involved in the conflict. Laboratory studies on health effects of depleted uranium exposure by medical researchers at the Swiss Institute of Technology (SIT, 2001) have shown that depleted uranium is carcinogenic, it causes tumors and DNA damage, crosses the blood-brain barrier and deposits in the brain, deposits in the lymph nodes and testes, and crosses the placenta and enters the fetus. The SIT findings suggest that ingested uranium found in Gulf veterans could not have come from natural sources as the military had claimed. The results of the SIT study on DU exposure indicate that depleted uranium cannot simply be naturally occurring uranium with the fissionable U-23.

Charatan's (2002) neurological research has focused on neurological diseases like amyotrophic lateral sclerosis (ALS), various malignant cancers, connective tissue diseases, and immunologic abnormalities to explain the undiagnosed illnesses of the Gulf veterans. Findings on the undiagnosed syndromes by the Presidential Advisory Committee on Gulf War Illnesses (PAC, 1996) final report also suggest Gulf War veterans' toxic exposures during the Gulf War resulted in discernible brain cell damage of some of the veterans. PAC findings suggests that some Gulf War veterans suffer from a pattern of health problems that significantly exceeds those seen in comparable populations, beyond that which is explained by stress or psychiatric diagnoses.

Most recent PAC (2004) report further mentioned that different epidemiological studies consistently show 25-30% of the veterans who served in the Gulf are ill, over and

The Human & Environmental cost of Wars

above the control population chosen for each study. The overall assessment of the PAC (2004, p. 19) study reads as follows:

> Heart rate measurements of gulf veterans show dysregulation of the autonomic nervous system in ill veterans. Gulf war veterans are suffering from ALS at approximately twice the expected rate. Audio-vestibular tests show abnormalities of central vestibular function. Ill veterans show elevated brain dopamine production. Risk factors associated with Gulf War Illnesses are present today in Southeast Asia. These risk factors include exposures to environmental toxins, low-level nerve agents, depleted uranium, oil fires and combinations of these factors.

Results of large National survey to determine pregnancy outcomes among United States Gulf War-era veterans by medical researchers Kang, Magee, et al.(2001, p.510-511) indicated Gulf war veterans reported a significant greater number of post-war pregnancies that ended in miscarriages or children born with birth defects than veterans who were not deployed. Among both male and female veterans, elevated rates were reported for all births defects combined, and for subsets of reported problems considered to most likely represent actual birth defects. In an earlier study, Kang and Bullman's (1996) documented mortality among United States veterans of the Persian Gulf War. In a follow-up study to their mortality study, Kang and Bullman (2000) focused on illness among United States veterans of the Persian Gulf War. In their initial epidemiological research Haley, Hom, Roland, et al. (1997) reported a possible increased number of birth defects and cancer in the civilian population of the Gulf War syndrome

Persian Gulf War. In their initial epidemiological research Haley, Hom, Roland, et al. (1997) reported a possible increased number of birth defects and cancer in the civilian population of the Gulf regions and southern Iraq. Haley and his associates reported three primary syndromes like symptom complexes identified as typical symptoms of Gulf War syndrome in a battalion of U.S. Naval Reserve construction troops. After a reexamination of the ill veterans, Haley and Kurt (1999) and his colleague documented that the use of armor and tanks for munitions as kinetic penetrators by the United States and British military forces presents a potential health risk when it enters the body as shrapnel or when inhaled following the aerosolization from impact and combustion due to its effects as a heavy metal and as a source of radiation.

The purpose of this book is to bring awareness to the long term human health and the environmental cost of wars by drawing attention to the concerns of servicemen and women, and civilians involved in recent military conflicts. The increased use of munitions containing depleted uranium in recent military conflicts has given rise to far broader questions regarding human health risks and environmental consequences. Investigations on human health issues and environmental hazards associated with these weapons have been conducted by numerous nuclear physicists and medical researchers in last decade. While reports by the United States Department of Defense and the United States government have suggests that the unexplained illnesses reported by servicemen and women deployed in the Balkans, the Persian Gulf and the Middle-East Gulf War were due to war time stress, counter reports available suggested otherwise.

Consistent findings from population-based studies of Gulf War era veterans have documented a wide range of symptoms at much significantly higher rates than non-Gulf

The Human & Environmental cost of Wars

veterans. There is now general consensus demonstrating excess morbidity in Gulf war veterans as a result of the large body of evidence.

2.2. The Use of Radioactive Waste in Military Weapons

The United States and other countries use the radioactive metal uranium-238, DU in military weapons systems. It is used in armor-piercing bullets, bomb casings, tank shielding, counterweights, and penetrators on missiles, and in cluster bombs, anti-personnel mines, and other anti-personnel weapons called dirt bombs. Beside uranium-238, depleted uranium also contains reprocessed nuclear waste which is itself highly toxic and radioactive. Weapons containing depleted uranium are appealing to military planners because of their pyrophoric qualities, which cause them to friction-burn on impact.

Medical and scientific findings have shown that when depleted uranium penetrators strike a hard target, they burn and create respirable-sized radioactive dust particles that have been known to contaminate surrounding soil, water, and flora and the human body. When explosives are also used, it disperses radioactive dust that poisons people and inflicts illness, injuries, and sometimes a lingering death. In an article in *Defense Watch,* a special report entitled "Countdown Iraq," Bob Nichols reports the 1991 casualties by the combined United States and NATO forces in Iraq and the Persian Gulf region. His report also mentioned the consequences of depleted uranium use on human health and the environment.

Further, in a summary report to the Intergovernmental Committee formed by the U.S. Congress to investigate Gulf War Related Illnesses (GWRI), the Presidential Advisory

The Human & Environmental cost of Wars

Committee (PAC 2002) informed the Congressional Committee members about the results of their findings. PAC findings indicates that Gulf War veterans suffer from a pattern of health problems that significantly exceeds those seen in comparable populations beyond that which is explained by stress or psychiatric diagnoses. It further mentioned that since the end of the Gulf War more than 200,000 of the more than 600,000 military service personnel deployed to the Persian Gulf have filed claims for veterans benefits based on service connected injuries and illnesses. The PAC report also mentioned that over 150,000 of the veterans who filed claims have been granted benefits.

A research paper published in the *American Journal of Public Health* (2005, p. 935) on Gulf War veterans indicates that service personnel may have been exposed to toxic and chemical agents during the March 1991 weapons demolitions in Khamisiyah, Iraq. This study's findings indicate that those veterans appear to have a higher risk for brain cancer death than veterans who were not exposed. The researchers compared causes of death among groups of Army Gulf War veterans who were possibly exposed to toxic substances to a group not exposed over a nine-year period and found no difference in overall mortality among exposed and non-exposed veterans. However, the study indicated that exposed veterans were about twice as likely to have died from brain cancer as unexposed veterans.

The Associated Press' August 12, 2006, internet archive indicated that since the end of the first Gulf War, about 30% of the 700,000 United States servicemen and women who were deployed during that war have registered in the Gulf War Illness database set up

The Human & Environmental cost of Wars

by the American Legion. According to this report, some of the Gulf War veterans still suffer a baffling array of serious health impairing symptoms. Furthermore, over 8,000 returning Gulf War veterans have died from Gulf War syndrome. Such figures create urgency as each new battle throughout the Middle East erupts.

The possibility that munitions containing depleted uranium are being used is very real. Scientific and medical researchers who have studied and examined the devastating effects of radioactive metal uranium -238, for instance, Rostker, (1998), Fetter, and Von Hippel (1999) and Durakovic (1999) have come to a general consensus that that the radioactive waste from the reactor fuel and the weapons-uranium refining process of natural uranium should be banned from military use.

Even though numerous medical and scientific studies have indicated that there are human health risks and environmental hazards associated with depleted uranium, nonetheless the United States Nuclear Regulatory Commission (USNRC, 1996) radioactive waste study on depleted uranium production argued that there are many commercial and non-military industrial and peaceful uses of depleted uranium that do not warrant a ban on the production of depleted uranium. USNRC radioactive waste study mentioned that leftovers from the use of nuclear materials which are radioactive wastes are used for the production of electricity, diagnosis and treatment of disease, and other purposes.

The USNRC study argued against a ban on the production of depleted uranium production stating that low-level radioactive wastes are used commercially as contaminated protective tools, clothing, filters, rags, medical tubes, and many other items. Furthermore,

The Human & Environmental cost of Wars

radioactive materials are used at medical facilities in numerous diagnostic and therapeutic procedures for patients. Radioactive materials are used in commercial and industrial firms to measure thickness, density, or volume of materials. It is used also to determine the age of prehistoric and geological objects, and to examine welds and structures for flaws. USNRC study indicates that radioactive materials are also used for oil and gas exploration and for various other types of research and development.

Other findings from the USNRC study suggests that, although natural uranium is a radioactive mineral, it only contains a small amount of the isotope U-235, that poses any actual human threat. It further indicates that it would require a greater quantity of isotopic concentrate for DU to pose a major health threat. There are some disagreements among some members of the scientific community about the safety of natural uranium use in commercial and industrial applications. Those opposed to depleted uranium's commercial or industrial uses are not convinced it is safe for humans or the environment. Opponents argued that both nuclear reactors and nuclear bombs require greater concentrations of U-235 to sustain a chain reaction. For example, those in the scientific community who seek a complete ban on DU for military and commercial uses.

Durakovic (1999) for instance, claimed depleted uranium radioactive wastes pose a health risk to humans and endangers the environment. However, other critics of depleted uranium military use, such as Cohen (1978), have argued, the use of depleted uranium in munitions has greater consequences for the proliferation of human and the environment.

The Human & Environmental cost of Wars

Depleted uranium is often used in armor penetrators when alloyed when depleted uranium is alloyed in military applications. The U.S. Army and NATO forces developed, tested, and fielded several weapons systems containing depleted uranium.

An independent report by Nick Cohen (*Independent on Sunday*, 10 Nov 1991) entitled, "Radioactive Waste Left in the Gulf by Allies," affirms that the U.S. Army is not the only country using depleted uranium. Cohen's report included the United Kingdom, Russia, Turkey, Saudi Arabia, Pakistan, Thailand, Israel, and France are countries actively engaged in developing weapons systems containing depleted uranium. According to Cohen's report, depleted uranium munitions are sold in the world market. Cohen's report is supported by the *Defense Trade News* (1992) statement that legislation in the U.S. made it permissible to sell the M-833 (or comparable anti-tank shells) containing depleted uranium penetrators to the following NATO countries: Belgian, Canada, Denmark, France, Germany, Greece, Iceland, Italy, Norway, Luxembourg, Netherlands, Portugal, Spain, Turkey, and the United Kingdom. It also cited United States sales to non-NATO countries, such as Australia, Egypt, Israel, Japan, Korea, and Taiwan.

2.3. World Depleted Uranium Inventory

Since the United States first led the world in using depleted uranium in 1991 during the Gulf War, the list of nations possessing or manufacturing depleted uranium weapons has rapidly grown. The list includes the United Kingdom, France, Russia, Greece, Turkey, Israel, Kuwait, Bahrain, Egypt, Thailand, Taiwan, Saudi Arabia, and Pakistan. United States Army Environmental Policy Institute (USAEP I1995, p.19-120) findings in a study

The Human & Environmental cost of Wars

on health and environmental consequences of depleted uranium uses, suggests that since DU weapons are openly available on the world arms market, depleted uranium weapons will be used in future conflicts. The USAEP study noted also that "the number of depleted uranium casualties on future battlefields probably will be significantly higher because other countries will use systems containing depleted uranium".

The proliferation of depleted uranium weapons in the arsenals of nations in some of the most volatile regions of the world is most likely to increase the numbers of depleted uranium exposures in future conflicts among friends and foe alike. Environmental Exposure Report entitled "Depleted Uranium in the Gulf", published by the U. S. Department of Defense (1998), suggests American soldiers and Marines are likely to be among the depleted uranium casualties on future battlefields. Depleted uranium's battlefield effectiveness has encouraged its steady proliferation.

Table 1 provides 1999 estimates of stocks of depleted uranium inventories in several locations around the world as presented by Joint Report of the Organization for Economic Co-operation and Development (OECD), the Nuclear Energy Agency (NEA), and the International Atomic Energy Agency (IAEA). The OECD, NEA and the IAEA jointly organized an expert group in 1999 for the assessment of the management depleted uranium and its potential uses. The report outlines current inventories of depleted uranium.

With an estimated 480,000kg of depleted uranium inventories in its stockpile, the United States has by far the largest inventory of depleted uranium, followed by Russia's

The Human & Environmental cost of Wars

depleted uranium stockpiles, which have been approximately 460,000kg; France has the third largest depleted uranium stockpiles in its inventories with approximately 190,000kg of depleted uranium. China, with 2,000kg, has the lowest number of depleted uranium in their inventories of all the five nuclear powers. Britain, with approximately 30,000kg, has the fourth largest depleted uranium stockpiles inventories. Germany has 16,000kg. Japan has 10,000kg uranium stockpile inventories.

Table 1 World Depleted Uranium Inventory as of the End of 1999.

Country	Organization	DU Stocks (000kg	Reported
USA	DOE	480,000	2002
Russia	FAEA	460,000	1996
France	COGEMA	190,000	2001
UK	BNFL	30,000	2001
Germany	URENCO	16,000	1999
Japan	JNFL	10,000	2001
Canada	CNNC	2,000	2000
South Korea	KAERI		2002
South Africa	NECSA	73	2001

The Human & Environmental cost of Wars

Total	1,188,273	2002

Source: OECD, NEA, 2001

The United Nations Environment Program (UNEP, 2001) published its findings of the first-ever assessment on the environmental impact of the use of depleted uranium originating from a real conflict situation in Kosovo in 2000, then in 2001 in Serbia and Montenegro. The United Nations Environmental Program has become a reference in the scientific community regarding the impacts of depleted uranium when used in a conflict situation. We have learned from this new United Nations Environmental Programme study that more than a decade after the end of the conflict in the Balkans, it is still possible to detect depleted uranium in soil and sensitive bio-indicators in sites where depleted uranium had been used. U. N. Environmental Programme (UNEP 2001, p.1) findings confirmed

> Large numbers of contamination points were depleted uranium penetrators hit the ground, as well as loose contamination, including depleted uranium penetrators, fragments and jackets/casings were found

The United Nations Environmental Programme findings in the Balkans made it possible for the first time to detect depleted uranium contamination in drinking water. The contamination, however, was very low and remained below the World Health Organization reference value. Depleted uranium was also detected in several of the air samples where it had been unexpected to find any depleted uranium particles in the air so long after the end of the conflict. The detected level, however, remained below the international safety limits. The possible health risks and questions of safe storage of radioactive waste were in-

The Human & Environmental cost of Wars

tegrated into the UNEP study of the assessment on the environmental impact of the use of depleted uranium originating from a real conflict. The UNEP environmental assessment team was composed of experts from the relevant United Nations agencies: the World Health Organization (WHO), and the International Atomic Energy Agency (IAEA).

In a detailed laboratory analysis of surface soil sample, the United Nations Environmental Programme assessment team revealed low levels of localized ground contamination. The finding of the United Nations Environmental Programme assessment team suggests that none of the bombing sites showed widespread contamination, meaning contamination over large surfaces in the range of a couple of hundred meters. The United Nations Environmental Programme assessment team finding suggests contamination of drinking water sample at one site, but only a trace of depleted uranium could clearly be identified in one drinking water sample. It also suggests that a trace of depleted uranium in a second drinking water sample was detectable only through the use of mass spectro-metric measurements.

The United Nations Environmental Programme assessment team findings indicate the presence of depleted uranium in air at two sites, but the concentrations were very low and resulting radiation doses were insignificant and minor. Overall, the U.N. Environmental Programme team assessment findings are consistent with its earlier depleted uranium studies. The United Nations Environmental Programme team final assessment on the environmental impact of the use of depleted uranium originating from a real conflict is that the levels of depleted uranium contamination are not a cause for alarm, but some uncertain-

ty remains with respect to future potential groundwater contamination from penetrators'
corrosion products.

In summary, this chapter introduced the human health risks and the environmental
hazards of the use of munitions containing depleted uranium in battlefields. It briefly discussed the etiological role of depleted uranium exposure in the genesis of Gulf War related
illnesses. It introduced varying epidemiological and scientific studies about the nature and
causes of the health problems affecting military service personnel and civilians since the
end of the Gulf War. It identified the complex set of challenges encountered by epidemio -
logists, researchers, government agencies, and the ill veterans who are trying to understand
and address the undiagnosed health conditions that have come to be known as Gulf War
Syndrome, which has been the subject of sustained controversy since the end of the Gulf
War. The next chapter will present a review of some of the scientific and medical literature
relating to DU toxicity.

CHAPTER 3

THE LITERATURE

3.1 Examination of the Relevant Literature on Depleted Uranium Toxicity

Medical and scientific researchers have not completely understood the full impact of the precise distribution and dynamics of internalized particles that depleted uranium oxide may have on the human body. Despite the lack of a complete understanding of the mechanisms by which damage to cells and organs occur, there is mountain of scientific evidence to indicate that uranium weapons are hazardous to human health and the ecosystem.

Evidence from scientific studies from both animal and in vitro studies suggests adverse effects on human health from inhaled depleted uranium particles through both radiological action and chemical toxicity. The carcinogenic, neutrotoxic, and immuno-toxic effects of depleted uranium, as well as its ability to damage the reproductive system and fetus, was shown in the results of Miller, Blakely, Livengood, Whittaker, et al. (1998) animal and cellular studies on the transformation of human osteoblast cells to the tumorigenic phenotype by depleted uranium-uranyl chloride.

Their animal cellular studies on the transformation of human of human Osteoblast cells demonstrate for the first time that malignant transformation of immortalized human cells can be achieved by exposure to the depleted uranium compound UO_2Cl_2. Chromosome aberration analysis in peripheral lymphocytes of Gulf War and Balkans War by Schroder, Heimers, Beyme, Schott, et al. (2003, p. 211) state that, "the UK Gulf War veterans and service personnel who had been deployed in the Balkans War have been exposed to internal radiation from depleted uranium particles."

Increasing levels of respiratory and cardiovascular diseases has been linked to exposure of fine particles. Samet, Dominici, Curriero, Coursac, et al. (2000) environmental exposure report linked mortality associated specifically with fine particles and particulate air pollution. Findings in Schwartz, Norris, Larson, Sheppard, et al. (1999) study of episodes of high coarse particles did not associate episodes of high coarse particle concentrations with increased mortality. Although, Schwartz and colleagues did not associate episodes of high coarse particle concentrations with increased mortality, Samet et al. (2000) study found that because of their small size fine particles can remain in the body for a longer period of time.

The high incidents of thyroid cancer were caused as a result of radiological weapons of high grade uranium isotopes. This finding has been confirmed in numerous medical and scientific studies. For instance, victims of nuclear and radiological terrorism study by Skorga, Persell and his colleagues (2003) found manifestations of radiation sickness, and identified hepato-cellular carcinoma as the most common type of liver tumor in victims exposed to toxicological substances and chemical agents. Fujikawa, Schizuma, Endo, et al. (2003) study of Japanese survivors documented evidence of somatic and genetic conse-

The Human & Environmental cost of Wars

quences resulting from exposure to contamination of uranium isotopes in a study of Nagasaki survivors.

The postwar hospitalization experience of U.S. Persian Gulf War veterans study by Gray, Coate, Anderson, Kang, Berg, Wignall, Knoke and Connor (1996), and Gray, Kaiser, Hawksworth, Smith, et al. (1999), to determine the prevalence of symptoms that may have been related to Gulf War hazards or other stressors was followed by a study of increased postwar symptoms and psychological morbidity among U.S. Navy Gulf War veterans by a cohort study on infertility among male U.K. veterans of the 1990-91 Gulf War by medical researchers Maconocchie, Doyle and Carson (2004). Their study was to assess whether the offspring of U.K. veterans of the first Gulf War are at increased risk of fetal or congenital malfunction indicate an increased incidence of some cancers in Gulf War veterans and congenital disorders in veterans' children. Although these studies did not specifically focus on the link between depleted uranium exposure and health damage of the United States and British veterans, their exposure to depleted uranium is thought to be a key factor in Gulf War Syndrome.

Hooper, Squibb, Siegle, McPhaul, and Keogh (1999) found elevated urine uranium excretion in their medical study of soldiers with retained uranium shrapnel among Gulf War veterans who had been wounded in friendly fire incidents. This study was to quantify body burdens of uranium over-time, and to detect any adverse health effects from exposure. The findings from this study indicate that embedded depleted uranium fragments could dissolve over time, and can potentially lead to toxic effects in the kidneys and other organs.

The Human & Environmental cost of Wars

McDiarmid, et al. (2000), in their study of comparative uranium Gulf War veterans who were wounded in friendly fire incidents with Gulf War veterans who were not exposed to uranium, showed that the veterans who were exposed to uranium had urinary levels as much as 600 times higher than the levels in the non-exposed group. However, the study of McDiarmid and his colleagues on health effects of depleted uranium on exposed Gulf War veterans did not show any association between urinary depleted uranium levels, kidney functions and proximal tubule damage, the type of kidney damage caused by high exposure in laboratory animals.

The test results of their study showed few uranium related clinical outcomes, but it revealed excrete elevated concentrations of urinary uranium in veterans who had embedded fragments. Early studies performed in 1991 by the Uranium Medical Research Center (UMRC 1991) the same year as Gulf War I, suggested evidence of the presence of uranium in the body and urine of veterans. Although the mechanism of mutagenicity, that is the capacity of a chemical or physical agent to cause permanent alteration of the genetic material within living cells and oncogenic effects of inhaled alpha particles, still remains unclear.

The practical implications of these studies are important in view of the fact that more than 10% of all cancer deaths in the United States are a result of pulmonary deposition of alpha emitters (Kennedy, Bruce, Ichiro, Prothrow-Smith, 1996). The lung remains the principal portal of entry of uranium isotopes into the internal environment of the body, and the skeletal tissue is the final target organ. Simon, Hickey, Fincher, Johnson, Ross, and

The Human & Environmental cost of Wars

Rea (1994) findings in a recent study of chronic exposure to natural uranium ore has been cited in many scientific and epidemiological studies as conclusive for both nonmalignant and malignant tumor risk in the lung.

The 1991 Persian Gulf War included an array of the 20th Century's most frightening and devastating weapons. Nuclear, chemical, and biological weapons were all poised for use, each with the ability to cause massive casualties among friends and foes alike. During the Gulf War, the United States and British forces introduced armor-piercing ammunition made of depleted uranium, a radioactive and toxic waste. The increasing use and eventual proli-feration of depleted uranium weapons ensure their part in armed conflict for the fore-seeable future. Accordingly, we must learn from the lessons of the use of depleted uranium weapons in the Gulf War and take steps to minimize and prevent the adverse effects on sol-diers, civilians, and food and water supplies. Established limits on intake of depleted uranium dust attest that just a small amount poses a serious health threat.

Evidence from the scientific literature on depleted uranium exposure and human health indicates that the route of depleted uranium intake in the body depends upon the me-thod of exposure (inhalation, ingestion, implantation, or wound contamination), and the size and solubility of the particles. The recent federally-sponsored Research on Persian Gulf Veterans' Illness (1997) reported that depleted uranium particles may remain in the lungs if inhaled or travel through the blood stream and deposit in the brain, bone, and reproductive Organs, kidney, muscles, and spleen.

The Human & Environmental cost of Wars

The report entitled, "A Summation of Test Data Pertaining to the Oxidation of Depleted Uranium during Battlefield Conditions (ARDEC 1991), indicates that insoluble depleted uranium particles (up to 83% by volume of the total dust created by impact), if inhaled, pose a radiological, as opposed to a chemical, toxicological hazard (ARDEC 8th March 1991, p.1). A risk assessment study by the United States Army Chemical School (USACS 1997) for imbedded depleted uranium fragments found the presence of depleted uranium in the semen of five of 22 American veterans who had been wounded by depleted uranium fragments in 1991.

Though additional studies on depleted uranium's health effects are needed, internalized DU is acknowledged by the Department of Veterans Affairs Gulf War Expert Scientific Advisory Committee (1998) to cause kidney damage, cancers of the lung and bone, non-malignant respiratory disease, skin disorders, neuron-cognitive disorders, chromosomal damage, and birth defects. There is a noted massive rise in cancers in Saudi Arabia and in most of the Emirates all the way to Bahrain. In calculable collateral damage to veterans, civilians, and neighboring Gulf States, now and for all future generations, is as a result of using radioactive weapons. Nuclear explosions cause massive damage at the time, while radioactive weapons cause more prolonged devastation to humans and the environment for tens of years may be, till the end of time since the half life of DU is the life of the solar system. All over the Persian Gulf areas, especially in the South in Iraq there has been a six-fold rise in cancers of all kinds, most especially leukemia and lymphomas.

The Human & Environmental cost of Wars

From being a rarity, birth defects have become so common that there can be three children in one family with birth defects. Plants and animals are also showing signs of the genetic mutation. Unborn children of the Gulf region are the ones who are going to pay the highest price of the health hazards of depleted uranium, and they will have to pay with the integrity of their DNA. Bosnia, Afghanistan, Saudi-Arabia, and Emirate countries such as Kuwait and other Persian Gulf states in the theater of international military conflicts in which DU was used, are showing similar health problems as the people in Iraq, who have been continually and constantly bombarded with depleted uranium since the initial bombing of 1991. Fifteen years after the end of Gulf War I, the people of Iraq and other surrounding Persian Gulf states have been experiencing significant increases in cancers, reproductive problems, and other strange mutative diseases.

An article in *Time Magazine,* (January 9, 2001*)* revealed that despite many studies saying that it is safe, a storm grows in NATO over the use of tank busting ammunition using nuclear waste. According to the article,

> The death from various cancers of at least 17 soldiers (15 of them from Leukemia) from European armies since being deployed on peace-keeping missions in Bosnia and Kosovo has raised an outcry in Europe, and some of their governments believe the cause of their illnesses may lie in the ammunition used by NATO against Serbian armor and artillery positions in both regions.

Several years after the end of Gulf War I, *Life Magazine* (July 1992) reporters Miller, Briggs, and Hudson state that "approximately 67% of the babies conceived by Gulf War Veterans after the war had severe birth defects." The children were shown to have been born with hands but no arms, no legs, organs on the outside of the body, missing organs,

32

and other deformities. These cluster cases have been identified as Goldenhar's Syndrome, a genetic disorder in which children are born with one side of their head shrunken, one ear and one eye working, and organs out of place. Pictures of the children show one small girl with benign tumors that were growing on the outside of her skin, and she needs laser surgery to shrink them.

According to Miller, Briggs, and Hudson (1992), since 1991, 67% of the babies are born with the same kind of deformities found in the plants and animals shown at Three Mile Island, as well as the deformities at Chernobyl, and in the military men who served during the Gulf Wars. (*Life Magazine,* July 1992). They wrote, "Iraqis with no family history of cancer are seeing entire families die because of the disease. Medical doctors have reported a rise in the rate of cancer as twelve times the rate before 1991 Gulf War."

Medical researchers are not able to explain the precise cause for the sudden increase in cancer rates and other depleted uranium elated diseases. Reasons for this include the restriction and lack of access to study those who have been exposed to DU, the inability to conduct a proper survey, or even to test the excess level of radiation in the victims' bodies. An article published in the *Time Magazine* (January 25, 2003) on human exposure to the dangers of the use of munitions containing depleted uranium by the U. S. and NATO troops during the Persian Gulf Conflict revealed that the "U. S. Army Environmental Policy Institute reported that more than 900,000 depleted uranium tipped bullets were fired.

The Human & Environmental cost of Wars

When they exploded, toxic substances were released in the ground and air and after four or five years, entered the food chain, affecting human lives. There are a number of medical and scientific scholarly reviews which have considered the many hazards caused by external radiation doses from depleted uranium. Some scholars (Fetter and Von Hippel, 1999) have used theoretical calculations and others have attempted direct measurements. Medical researchers in Britain's Royal Society (RS, 2001) who have studied human exposure to depleted uranium have suggested that depleted uranium exposure could occur in unprotected handling of the depleted uranium munitions, such as loading and working with depleted uranium munitions, and in handling fragments of these munitions.

These scholars estimated that the theoretical maximum whole-body gamma-ray dose-rate from external exposure to depleted uranium munitions in a uranium store or in a vehicle reinforced by depleted uranium containing armor and armed with its complement of depleted uranium is 0.025mSv per hour. They suggest dose rates in this range may be experienced by a person completely surrounded by depleted uranium ammunitions.

At the end of the Balkans conflict, the WHO (2001) calculated the amount of depleted uranium deposited at an average attack site in Kosovo. The WHO study demonstrated that if all the depleted uranium munitions expended during an attack remained within one kilometer, the increase of uranium in the soil would be 5%. The additional contribution of depleted uranium from military use to background radiation dose in Kosovo is within the natural variations found for background levels. The WHO (2001) report suggests that picking up a penetrator and keeping it in a pocket is the only realistic way to maintain a long period of exposure to external (beta) radiation from depleted uranium.

The available evidence from some European nuclear researchers indicates that external contact with depleted uranium in tact penetrators or as uranium oxide dust does not convey an appreciable excess adverse health risk when a hard target, such as an armored tank or a rocky outcrop, is hit by depleted uranium munitions. A report from the Office of the Special Assistant for Gulf War Illnesses (2000) indicates that a proportion of the original depleted uranium metal (usually 10%-35%, up to a maximum of 70%) forms an aerosol of the metal and its combustion products, which are predominantly uranium oxides. The report indicates that aerosols and dusts containing DU and its oxides may be inhaled into the lungs, but based on particle size; the report estimated that about 60%-69% of the aerosolized fraction of such a proportion of the original depleted uranium is respirable.

A United Nations Environmental Programme (1999) study conducted on the consequences of the Kosovo conflict on the environment concluded that an acute hazard from inhaled uranium aerosols is related to the extent and rate of transfer of inhaled uranium to the blood and the presumed amounts reaching the primary targets in the kidney. In a post-conflict environmental assessment study at the end of the Kosovo conflict, The United Nations Environmental Programme (UNEP, 2001) estimated that the inhalation and ingestion of depleted uranium contaminated dust, even under extreme conditions, shortly after the impact from projectiles would be less than 10 mSv. That estimation is based on the amount

The Human & Environmental cost of Wars

of dust that can be inhaled under those conditions. This amount represents about half the annual dose limit for radiation workers.

The United Nations Environmental Programme study indicates that for people in open areas near the theater of war where tanks were destroyed or were near burning depleted uranium, the aerosol dose is less over time considerably, and the potential exposure is further reduced by climatic influences, such as rain or snow. The study also indicates that food may become a vehicle for uptake of depleted uranium. Plants may take up uranium from the soil and may adhere to the root surface. A study conducted by the European Commission on Depleted Uranium, Nuclear Safety and Civil Protection (2001) indicates that consumption of 100 kg/year of vegetables grown in soil with 70 mg of depleted uranium per kilogram of soil would yield a radiation dose of 0.0026 mSv/year.

The study concluded that consumption of unwashed roots and vegetables may increase exposure due to ingestion of soil washing, it claims, will reduce soil intake by 99%. The World Health Organization (WHO, 2001) exposure and health effect study on depleted uranium munitions on the environment indicates that it is known that aquatic macrophytes accumulate uranium, and there are species of plants in the Alligator River region of Australia that show preferential concentration of uranium. The World Health Organization (2001) mission in Kosovo explored the theory that uranium dust might become incorporated in vegetables and crops. The mission was advised by an agency of the United Nations, the Food and Agricultural Organization (FAO) that in the published literature there are yet, no known (cultivated) plants that preferentially accumulate uranium, and the normal amounts of uranium taken up in plants would not be expected to be dangerous to humans, birds, or other animals.

The impact of chemicals on the environment and human health is a cause of increasing concern. Although many studies continue to be carried out on this subject, most address only individual chemicals or particular groups of chemicals, such as metals or radioactive substances. Radioactive substances, including naturally occurring radio-isotopes and its decay products and processed materials, such as depleted uranium, affect the environment and human health because of their radiological and chemical toxicity. This is a growing worldwide awareness of relationships between the ecosystem and human health, and the distribution of chemicals in the environment (RCEP, 2003).

There is also an increasing realization by medical research scholars, Skinner and Berger (2003), that although geo-hazards, such as volcanoes and earthquakes, are dramatic and cause sudden significant loss of life, the threat from chemicals, which is frequently insidious, can cause even greater loss of life, the threat from chemicals, which is frequently insidious, can cause even greater loss of life and debility over longer term.

The problem of chronic exposure to potentially toxic chemicals in the environment is also articulated by the European Environment Agency and the United Nations Environment Programme (EEA/UNEP, 1999). Radioactivity may also be introduced into the environment as a result of contamination from a wide range of anthropogenically produced radionuclide including the manufacture, testing, and use of nuclear weapons, nuclear acci-

The Human & Environmental cost of Wars

dents and, to an equal extent, the use of ammunition containing depleted uranium in military conflicts. Since the development, manufacture, and the use of ammunition containing depleted uranium into military conflicts, hazardous chemicals have been released into the atmosphere and the natural environment as water, soil, and airborne contaminants. The scientific understanding of depleted uranium's effect on health is still evolving.

In summary, this chapter began with a review of some of the relevant literature relating to munitions containing depleted uranium, and the health risks and environmental hazards caused by such exposures.

The next chapter will continue with various epidemiological and scientific perspectives on the controversies of depleted uranium and other substances exposure and their health implications. It further discussed some of the epidemiological and scientific differences and perspectives relating to uranium and toxic and chemical exposures. The next chapter outlines the procedures, methods, and theoretical approach used in this research to explore and understand the social world of the Gulf War veterans who were ill as a result of exposure to depleted uranium.

CHAPTER 4

METHODOLOGY

This study utilizes a naturalistic approach to provide new insights, meaning and description as it seeks to illustrate, understand and interpret or explain about the day-to-day life experiences and structures from the perspectives of the Gulf War veterans. It is focused on a naturalistic inquiry because it contains data extracted from live interviews given by Gulf War veterans and non-military personnel exposed to depleted uranium. A purposive sampling method was used to select the documentary materials for analysis in this study. To help me become familiar with the basic facts of the human health risks and environmental hazards of the use of munitions containing depleted uranium in the battlefields, the first phase in this study was to conduct a search in the internet using a search engine.

The first step in my familiarization process about depleted uranium use started with a search in Google search engine. I entered the depleted uranium use in Google; it gave me 2,080,000 entries on depleted uranium use. I meticulously skimmed through the first 50 articles, and then select the first 25 articles from the huge number of possible articles. Then I typed in Human health hazards of depleted uranium use; it gave me 301,000 entries. From these huge entries, I patiently skimmed through every other 30 articles, 15 articles were se-

The Human & Environmental cost of Wars

lected from the entries. I then typed in Depleted uranium weapons, it gave me 1,590,000 entries from which to select from.

I skimmed through the 25 articles, 15 of those articles were thoroughly reviewed, and 10 articles were selected from the entries. I then typed in depleted uranium ammunitions; it gave me 409,000 entries from which I selected the first five articles. I typed in depleted uranium in the Gulf War, it gave me 887,000 entries. I examined the first 10 articles and every other 20 articles after that; I selected eight articles on depleted uranium use in the Gulf War. I then typed in depleted uranium and environmental Hazards; it gave me 373,000 entries. I selected the first five articles and thoroughly examined them for contextual significance. Then, I typed in Gulf War and undiagnosed Illnesses, it gave me 46,700 entries. I selected the first of every 25 articles and examined them for their contextual significance. I then search several database for scholarly journals on articles relating to depleted uranium use health effects, and environmental hazards. I started with JSTOR, it gave me eight entries, and I selected all eight entries and examined them thoroughly for context. I selected the eight articles and read, and re-read them and to get a better understanding of depleted uranium use its effects on human health and the damages it causes to the environment.

I then searched the major newspapers and magazine internet achieves for stories relating to depleted uranium and the Gulf War Illnesses. I searched through *The New York Times* internet achieves for stories on Gulf War veterans related illnesses. I then searched other leading newspapers such as the *Seattle Inquirer, the Guardian, the Nation, the Inde-*

The Human & Environmental cost of Wars

pendent Britain, the Independent on Sunday, the Guardian, U.S. News and World Report. I also searched through *Time and Life* magazines for stories to help me understand the effects of depleted uranium on human health from the experiences of Gulf War veterans and civilians in their own words as reported and published in newspapers and magazines.

I believe all the articles from the internet search engines, the newspapers, magazines and all the other selected document materials has given me information about United States Military and Government responses to their complaints and their health problems. I was also interested in any reports of scientific analyses of health effects and environmental pollution. I see myself as an observer who is particularly interested in understanding the social construction and resulting controversy of how veterans, military doctors, military officials and governments' representatives come to terms with veterans' reports of, in some cases, life threatening illnesses which may have been caused their exposure to hazardous amounts of depleted uranium products of military weapons systems used on the battlefield. It is my interest in the social construction of these events that guided my categories of themes.

Grounded theory is the methodological approach employed in this study to describe and to explain the experience and meaning of the Gulf War syndrome in the lives of veterans who were deployed in the Gulf war. It will also provide a method to identify explanatory themes critical to understanding the relationships among depleted uranium munitions, human health risks, environmental hazards, and various mitigation strategies. In the tradition used by qualitative researchers (Glaser & Strauss, 1967; Strauss & Corbin, 1990),

The Human & Environmental cost of Wars

this study will assess the data and analysis which have been collected from newspapers, magazines, and electronic media reports.

Grounded theory is typified by simultaneous data generation and analysis, and the use of intensive analytic processes that include constant comparison, levels of coding, and theoretical sampling. Central to this exploratory study is to understand the experiences and the frame of mind of the veterans and civilians exposed to depleted uranium. The thematic analysis of the documentary materials is analyzed to evaluate specific illnesses that may have resulted from deployment to the Arabian Gulf and the possibility of a new or previously unrecognized syndrome.

Social constructionism is the theoretical framework used in this study. As adopted and articulated by Berger and Luckman (1966, p. 15), this theoretical framework recognizes the social involvement of the Gulf War veterans within a social context for meaning gained through retrospective and emergent contexts. In this study, social constructionism is used to explore how meanings and understandings of the veterans exposed to depleted uranium grew out of their experiences with weaponry under battlefield conditions. I have collected news- paper and magazine articles, electronic media reports, document achieves, reports from theInternet and congressional committees and sub-committee reports.

The data collected from these sources have been closely read. Significant statements from the documentary materials were extracted, coded, and grouped thematically to help to identify analytic domains. This analytic strategy is to help me organize the data within broad themes. I used the method of constant comparative analysis to group statements supporting both sides of the arguments related to the effect of weapon-grade depleted uranium.

Information within each thematic category was subsequently evaluated to define the boundaries and relevance of each of the major themes. This process of bracketing thematic categories has allowed me to find points of tension and conflict, and to discard what does not fit within the objective of the study. The systematic process of coding allowed the theory to emerge from the data as written in the collected documents. This qualitative approach opened the possibilities for uncovering the meaning of Gulf War-related illnesses to veterans and their families.

The social constructionist theoretical framework, articulated by Taylor and Bodgan (1984, 1998), is used in this study and communicated through concepts extracted from data in the document materials. As adopted by Zanieuki (1934), analytic induction allows me to modify the social concepts and relationships between concepts. The goal is to accurately represent the reality of the Gulf War veterans' situation. As articulated by Glaser & Strauss (1967), this method allows me to scan and to identify the data collected from the document materials into categories and attributes. It helps me to create typologies for the categories in the data and to provide a means for arriving at a fit among the data extracted from document materials and to determine the relationships that exist, and to help me make constant comparative analysis and to briefly describe and contrast the method of analysis the theory produced.

The Human & Environmental cost of Wars

Finally, strategies for mitigating the effects of depleted uranium munitions on human health risks and environmental hazards are based on reports from United States Nuclear Regulatory Commission (USNRC), the United States Environmental Protection Agency (USEPA), and the European Environment Agency (EEA), and the World Health Organization (WHO). The emergency management mitigation strategies are from an approach which includes long term planning, policy development, and implementation. These strategies, mostly needed by emergency management in fighting against chemical and radiological toxic disasters, such as exposure to depleted uranium, are often neglected.

Past lessons from Three Mile Island (TMC) and Chernobyl have taught us that to prevent future disasters of the magnitude of those two technological disasters, we have to first and foremost restructure our national policy on disaster management to reflect the holistic approach, which should involve prevention, mitigation, and preparedness in pre-disaster phase with appropriate additional funding, along with the existing policy of post-disaster relief and rehabilitation under emergency management crisis management mitigation.

In summary, this chapter outlines methods, theory, and procedures used to conduct this research. Procedures for data collection and analysis were recounted herein. The next chapter will present the thematic analysis of the data gathered in this study. The next chapter presents the thematic analysis that emerged from document materials.

CHAPTER 5

THEMATIC ANALYSIS

The debate over the human health risks and the environmental hazards from the use of munitions containing depleted uranium continues. The issue first surfaced in the spring of 1999, when the U. S. and NATO military forces intervened in the Yugoslavia. There is little consensus in the medical and scientific communities about consequences of depleted uranium use on human health and the environment. Nuclear experts, medical and scientific scholars, conservative and liberal journalists, and laypersons alike have generally agreed that depleted uranium is at the very least toxic as well as radioactive.

The data for analysis in this study are derived from document materials extracted from newspaper and magazine articles, electronic news, documents archives, and internet reports of special Congressional committee hearings. This analytic strategy has helped in organizing the data within broad themes. Six themes that have emerged through analytic induction have been grouped and categorized within their interpretation into two thematic categories health risks and environmental hazards. The following are the health risk and environmental hazards themes which have emerged through analytic induction:

1.   Medical uncertainties

2.   Unresponsive medical system

3. Contamination of the natural resources and the environment

4. Environmental and health consequences

5. Unexplained physical symptoms

6. Long lasting unexplained physical symptom

Medical uncertainties is a theme which has emerged from the documentary materials as a factor involving the diagnostic legitimacy of veterans exposed to the unusual illnesses that the medical communities have nicknamed Gulf War Syndrome. Medical certainty is perceived as a prerequisite for diagnostic legitimacy, for it gives diagnostic legitimacy in the medical community. It also provides the basis for understanding by the lay community. Furthermore, medical certainty is frequently a prerequisite to mobilize whatever resources are necessary to combat the disease. Absence of diagnostic legitimacy in the medical community created an impediment for diagnosis of the illnesses that were plaguing the veterans exposed to depleted uranium or other chemical agents.

Larry Johnson editorialized in the *Seattle Post-Intelligencer* that "depleted uranium weapons used as a prime suspect for the Gulf War Syndrome that has sickened and killed thousands of U. S. veterans" (*The Seattle Post-Intelligencer*, August 4, 2003). Six years prior to Johnson's editorial, Dr. Robert Haley, an epidemiologist at the University of Texas Southwestern Medical Center, had claimed to have established an association between various chemical exposures and certain symptoms clusters as perceived by Gulf War veterans.

The Human & Environmental cost of Wars

Unresponsive medical system is an emergent theme which relates to how those veterans and their families who were exposed to depleted uranium perceived their experiences. For those who are suffering from the unexplained symptoms caused by their exposure to chemical agents, a diagnosis would have provided them some comfort through having a name to give to the unusual illnesses they were experiencing. Diagnosis by the medical community would have provided a legitimization that their medical complaints were taken seriously by the Defense Department and the American people at large.

Contamination of the natural resources and the environment is one of many themes on environmental justice which have emerged from general categorization of the documentary materials in this study. Alex Kirby published a story in *The Guardian* (March 22, 2000) in which he attributed the use of depleted uranium in Kosovo to cancer -causing agents. Kirby's report was dismissed by United States and British military authorities, claiming that the risk was minimal, if there was any risk at all. According to Kirby, the NATO Secretary-General, Lord Robertson, wrote a letter to Secretary-General of the United Nations, Kofi Annan, saying, "DU rounds were used whenever the A-10aircraft engaged armor during operation Allied Force. Therefore, it was used throughout Kosovo during approximately 100,000 missions, a total of approximately 31,000 rounds of depleted uranium ammunitions were used."

Chris Hedges, writing in the *New York Times* (July 14, 1999), described farm workers who, after plunging their fingers into the earth, said they came away with rashes that burn and blister. He wrote,

The Human & Environmental cost of Wars

Not only was the earth contaminated with toxic materials, but, also, were the rivers. Those who eat the fish from the river, the vegetables planted in the soil, or drink the tap water from the faucets, come down with illnesses such as diarrhea, vomiting and stomach ache.

Environmental and health consequences theme emerges from targeting of industrial and military sites and oil factories, actions which pose health and environmental consequences. The report from UNEP on the Kosovo war concluded that the American and NATO military forces action resulted in no ecological catastrophes. Nonetheless, the UNEP report regarded the bombing actions using ammunition tipped with depleted uranium as resulting in some serious hot spots in which hazardous substances released during the air strikes posed a risk for human health and the aquatic environment.

The environmental and health consequences themes were identified in documentary materials which claim that American and NATO forces damaged the environment by dropping 10,000-ton bomb munitions tipped with depleted uranium by air strikes. Further more, articles related the environmental damage to the burning and destruction of the oil wells and refineries by the defeated Iraqi forces as they retreated from Kuwait. These documentary articles reported that retreating Iraqi forces destroyed more than 700 oil wells in Kuwait, spilling an estimated 60 million barrels of oil.

Following the conclusion of the Gulf war, reports of unusual illnesses that were later dubbed Gulf War-related illnesses by the medical community began to mount. Gulf War veterans and their families stated that they were exposed to munitions tipped with depleted uranium and other chemical agents. Members of the U. S. Congress began to question the

The Human & Environmental cost of Wars

U. S. Department of Defense (DOD) assertions that no U.S. servicemen were exposed to chemical agents and no chemical agents had been detected during the war.

The DOD officials in the Pentagon became wary as the media began to report claims of chemical agent detections and chemical agent exposure by Czechoslovak troops who served in the Persian Gulf War. The issue of low-level chemical exposure was addressed in a report presented in September 1998 by the General Accounting Office (GAO).

Documentary material used in the analysis which relates to the theme of **medical uncertainties** emerges from claims of medically unexplained symptoms reported by U.S. servicemen who were deployed to the Persian Gulf. Those medical uncertainties resemble multiple chemical sensitivities, symptoms similar to fibromyalgia, and chronic fatigue syndromes. The other unusual illnesses included memory loss, fatigue, joint pain, dermatitis, headaches, blurred vision, diarrhea, and other symptoms. The U.S. veterans were not the only servicemen who were experiencing these unusual illnesses. Numerous veterans from multiple nations also began experiencing symptoms for which many of them had sought help.

At the conclusion of the 1991 Gulf War, American veterans and veterans from NATO countries who were deployed to the Persian Gulf region began experiencing symptoms for which they sought help in hospitals in the United States, Britain, and other NATO countries. In the context of medical care, American Gulf war veterans seldom received any diagnosis at all for the symptoms they were experiencing. Gulf war veterans who received the diagnosis of Gulf War Syndrome from their physicians received little satisfaction. They were told there symptoms were stress related. An increasing number of veterans who complained about their symptoms were told their mysterious diseases were not traceable to known pathogens or toxins.

Unexplained physical symptoms are interpreted by veterans as a major reason why they failed to receive medical treatment. The theme of *environmental pollution and health hazard* is interpreted as responsible for the increased risk of birth defects. Long lasting health effects is a theme used for describing mercury and dioxins being washed into the Danube. Another reason why the Gulf veterans were having difficulties in receiving treatment for their symptoms was because of disputes over the definition and etiology of their symptoms. As a result of medical uncertainty, and the failure of the sufferers of the symptoms to gain diagnostic legitimacy in the medical community, they were unable to receive the care they believed they needed.

Reports on the environmental hazards of munitions containing depleted uranium first began to surface in Bosnia and Herzegovina at the end of the Yugoslavia war in 1999, when American and NATO forces intervened in the Bosnian conflict. In the United States, David Holley's article (*The New York Times*, October 27, 1999) brought the nation's attention to the urgent steps needed to clean up the environmental damage created by American and NATO bombing of Yugoslavia using munitions containing depleted uranium.

The Human & Environmental cost of Wars

In Holley's *New York Times* article on the environmental damage caused by American and NATO bombing, "U. N. urges cleanup of 'Hot Spots' left by Kosovo War," Holley failed to mention any direct relationship between the environmental damage and pollution caused by the release of low-level uranium contained in the hundreds of tons of bombs dropped during the Bosnian conflict by American and NATO forces. Holley writes, "The United Nations observers who urge the cleanup of the bombing sites in Yugoslavia did not believe that the bombing by American and NATO forces during the war caused as much environmental damage, they suggests that 70% of the pollution had existed there before the bombing started."

Holley also cited a study sponsored by UNEP and the Human Settlement team, but concluded that it did not find any conclusive evidence of environmental pollution. However, evidence showed that the American and NATO forces' 78-day bombing campaigns released enough pollutants to increase the risk of birth defects among the fetuses of pregnant women. *Environmental pollution and health hazard* is a theme which emerged from the UNEP and Human Settlement team report.

United Nations teams of observers who visited the pollution sites in Bosnia at the end of the war blamed much of the pollution in the Danube River from upstream sources and outdated technology used in factories during the 10 to 15 years before the Balkan conflict, and for not following environmental - management development. This finding is similar to that reported by Holley (*New York Times* 1999) on the UNEP and Human Settlement team, which also found no evidence in Yugoslavia of radioactivity caused by American and NATO forces' use of ammunition tipped with depleted uranium.

A long and lasting health effect is another theme which has emerged from newspaper articles about data on the threatening pollution of depleted uranium on the environment. Paul Brown's article in *The Guardian* (Oct. 27, 1999) which talks about Pancevo, one of worst hit areas during the war in Yugoslavia, recounts the hazards facing people living on the Danube River in which mercury and dioxins have been detected. Furthermore, these life threatening conditions were spread downstream through drinking water in Bulgaria and Rumania. Brown wrote, "The environmental and health hazards which resulted from the American and NATO

forces bombing using ammunition tipped with depleted uranium will have a long and lasting effect on those populations for time to come."

Joe Laura, (*The Globe* Aug. 6, 1999), wrote about the contamination sites caused by the American and NATO troops bombing that were revealed in the United Nations Environmental Program/Habitat Balkans Task Force (UNEP/HBTF). The head of the Task Force, a former Finish environmental minister claimed, "The bombing of industrial sites during the Balkans war has caused very serious environmental and probably also serious health consequences."

Laura further claimed that investigators of the UNEP/HBTF were also able to find asbestos and other toxic substances in the surrounding soil in several of the 15 industrial

The Human & Environmental cost of Wars

sites hit by the American and NATO bombardment. He wrote, "The effects on the human health and the environment from the bombing of the American and NATO forces on the industrial sites during the Yugoslavia war had been enormous; more than 100,000 tons of carcinogens were unleashed into the air, the water and the soil" (*The Globe* Aug. 6, 1999).

The environmental and health hazard conditions in the aftermath of the 1991 Gulf War stimulated an on going search for etiological explanation. Two years before the United States and NATO troops' invasion of Iraq, Julie Flint (*The Daily Star*, September 14, 2004) wrote that a report commissioned by World Health Organization (WHO) had warned that the use of depleted uranium would have long-term damage on the health of Iraq's civilian population. She cited a WHO report written by three of Europe's top radiation scientists, including Dr. Keith Baverstock, one of WHO's leading expert on radiation and health for more than a decade. She wrote, "Dr. Baverstock believes, had the study been published in November of 2001, there would have been more pressure on the Allies to limit their use of depleted uranium DU during the invasion of Iraq and to clean up afterward, but it wasn't published" (*The Daily Star*, Sep. 14, 2004).

The lingering health concerns and birth defects was a leading story in Seattle's major newspapers (*The Seattle Post-Intelligencer*, August 4, 2003). Writing from the Baghdad office for the *Seattle Post-Intelligencer*, foreign desk editor Larry Johnson wrote, "Depleted uranium which is a toxic as well as radioactive, is at the very least a potential cause of cancers and birth defects." In his editorial, Johnson echoed the views of many Iraqi physicians and other nuclear experts that the United States and the Allied-led NATO forces are to blame for a major increase of cancers and birth defects that have occurred a few years after the 1991 and subsequent Iraqi war.

The theme of long lasting health effects was evident from as early as six years prior to the *Seattle Post* article. Dr. Robert Haley, when asked (PBS Frontline, October 1997) about his view on Gulf War Syndrome, replied that he was convinced there is a real Gulf War Syndrome. Dr. Haley stated that "among the 24th Navy Mobile Construction Battalion that we studied, there were 30 syndromes; they are very strong and they are due to neuro-logical damage and they are strongly associated with combinations of organic phosphate chemical exposures." However, Dr. Haley's Gulf Syndrome study was criticized by a number of epidemiologists because, in their view, the study contained bias in that not all of the members of the battalion participated in the study. Some of Dr. Haley's critics accused him of using the wrong neurological tests for organophosphate induced delayed neuropathy.

Since the media's focus is not only on what epidemiologists have come to define as the Gulf War Syndrome, but also on the person with the syndrome, it has helped the American people understand Gulf War-related illnesses. Haley (PBS Frontline, 1997) spoke about the human side of his epidemiological findings. He said,

> "This human aspect approach taken by both the print and television media has compelled the American public to start paying keen interest to the health and well-being of those men and women who have sacrificed their lives and those of their families in service of the nation as a whole."

However, while veterans with unexplained symptoms continued to seek attention, the media continued to raise issues. Larry Johnson's *Seattle Post-Intelligencer* (August 4,

The Human & Environmental cost of Wars

2003, p. A1) article entitled "War's unintended effects: use of depleted uranium weapons lingers as health concern." It focused on the abnormally high levels of radiation and environmental contamination throughout Iraq caused by depleted uranium weapons used by the United States-led forces during the Gulf War.

Johnson wrote that the *Seattle Post Intelligencer* conducted tests in six sites from Basra to Baghdad to see whether they could discover any evidence of remnants of radioactive materials in those sites some 12 years after the end of the first Gulf War. Johnson reported,

> They found elevated levels of radiation at all of the six sites they visited; one destroyed tank near Baghdad was 1,500 times more radioactive than normal background radiation. In other sites, the paper reported that investigators their discovered 1,400 times more radioactive than normal background.

Johnson's article resonates with the theme of *contamination of the natural resources and the environment.*

There are many newspaper and magazine articles written in the United States, Britain, and elsewhere that makes claims and provides stories of veterans and family members were sustaining health effects that include high incidences of birth defects in their offspring. Such claims include incidences of leukemia and other undiagnosed health problems as a result of exposure to the toxic and radioactive waste released from munitions containing depleted uranium. A prompt response by the medical community would have provided an official label for their illness, and would have legitimized the complaints of the veterans and other sufferers exposed to depleted uranium and other chemical agents.

The Human & Environmental cost of Wars

Various journalists attempted to fill in the gap between the veterans and the official medical response. Again, they wrote stories reporting *long lasting unexplained symptoms*. An article on severe birth defects among children of women in the local unit of the National Guard in Jackson, Mississippi, which appeared in *The Nation* (March 7, 1994) entitled, "Mal de Guerre" by Laura Flanders, stirred up controversies between those claiming that the birth defects were a result of depleted uranium exposures and those who argued that there were no relationships between the two.

Flanders wrote, "Among women in the local unit of the National Guard severe birth defects affected thirteen of fifteen babies conceived by veterans or their spouses since the end of the Gulf war" (*The Nation*, March 7, 1994). She continued, "67% of the children of 25 parents who participated in a Veterans Administration (VA) statewide survey revealed the children they conceived since the end of the war were afflicted with illnesses rated severe or have birth defects including missing eyes and ears, blood infections, respiratory problems, and fused fingers." The results of the statewide survey cited in Flanders's article resonate with the theme of *medical uncertainties* involving diagnostic legitimacy in the medical community.

Immediately after Laura Flanders's controversial article on birth defects among the children of veterans appeared in *The Nation,* the VA went on the offensive to discredit her story. Instead of launching an investigation to find out what was happening to the children of women, the VA criticized Flanders. They accused her of fabrication and of not providing

The Human & Environmental cost of Wars

any references to support statements in her article. The VA argued that they had found no reports to support Flanders's claims. The attacks on Flanders's article by the VA resonate with the theme of *unresponsive medical system.* Several months after the publication of Flanders's article, Richard Serrano, a reporter for the *Los Angeles Times* (*Nov.* 14, 1994) published a story on a new generation of birth defects in Gulf veterans' babies. Serrano's story was about a daughter of Gulf veterans from West Waynesboro, Mississippi, who had been born prematurely with collapsed lungs and a faulty immune system, and the son of another Gulf veteran who was constantly suffering from strange colds, pneumonia, and high fevers.

Serrano *(Los Angeles Times,* Nov. 1994*).* wrote:These are just a couple of the Gulf War's second-generation causalities; there are many others, including children who are dying of heart defects, liver diseases, and other rare disorders in Waynesboro, Mississippi, which was the site of the National Guard quartermaster corps, 13 out of 15 children born to Gulf veterans suffers from serious disorders (Los Angeles Times, Nov. 14, 1994).

Serrano also cited the testi -mony of Dr. Ellen Silbergeld, a molecular toxicologist at the University of Maryland, at a congressional hearing about the rising number of birth defects among children of Gulf War veterans. Dr. Silbergeld testified in a Congressional sub-committee hearing that "men can pass toxic chemicals on to their unborn children through their semen Dr. Silbergeld's testimony resonates with the theme of *long lasting unexplained physical symptoms.*

In addition, Serrano's article also contained a story of the wives of Gulf War veterans who claimed that they have been sexually affected by the symptoms that were affecting their ill husbands. In an interview with Ted Koppel of *ABC TV News Nightline*, Betty Mekdeci, founder of the Association of Birth Defect Children, confirms the occurrence at an alarming and disproportional rate of Goldenhar's syndrome in Gulf veterans' offspring. She declared that the type of problem most frequently reported to her organization in connection with the offspring veterans is related "chronic, serious immune problems" (Dec. 27, 1995).

Yet, responses from the military doctors to the veterans were not forthcoming. This lack of medical response repeatedly generated the theme, *unresponsive medical system.* Cary, Peter, and Tharp's article entitled "Gulf War's Grave Aura," *U. S. News and World Report* (July 8, 1996, p. 33-34) resonated with the theme of *unexplained physical symptoms.* Cary, Peter, and Tharp's article attempted to disprove connections between Gulf War veterans' illnesses and exposure to munitions containing depleted uranium hazardous waste.

They wrote,

The term Gulf War Syndrome is not one, easily defined problem, but rather encompasses a wide variety of ailments; Army reservist whose Army reserve unit was stationed at a prisoner of war camp in the region feels that Gulf War Syndrome is really a misnomer.

The second phase in the methodological approach in this study was to explore and analyze reports presented to the sub-committees- of the Senate Veterans Affairs for Gulf War Illnesses hearings, and testimonies and reports of the special investigations unit on

The Human & Environmental cost of Wars

Gulf War Illnesses presented to the Sub Committee on Banking and Governmental Affairs in the U.S. House of Representatives. The testimonials presented during the sub-committee hearings resonate with the themes of *medical uncertainties* and *unexplained physical symptoms* in relating to the strange, but very dangerous and life threatening illnesses occurring among Gulf War veterans and their families.

U. S. News and World Report (July 8, 1996, p. 33-34) published a story about Steven Bayer, a former Army reservist and now a congressman from Indiana who claimed to have experienced some of the symptoms of the Gulf War Syndrome firsthand. "Bayer claimed that the heightened frequency of illnesses among veterans is due to the wide variety of hazardous substances that they encountered in the Gulf regions." Bayer's battlefield experience with depleted uranium resonates with the theme of *environmental and health consequences..* His claim is supported by much of what other Gulf War veterans have reported.

Shenon Philip (*The New York Times*, Dec. 3, 1996, pp. 1, 16) wrote a story which claimed that chemical warfare detector alarms were going off at bases across the Gulf region during the Gulf War, and the chairman of the Joint Chiefs of Staff, Colin Powell, denied any evidence of any use of toxic chemicals during the Gulf War. However, Philip wrote,

> Many Gulf War veterans who testified before the United States Congressional Committee for Gulf War Related Illnesses claimed that chemical warfare detector alarms at bases across the region were frequently triggered, yet troops were ordered to ignore the alarms.

The Human & Environmental cost of Wars

This inconsistency between the U.S. Army and evidence presented in testimonies before the sub-committees on Gulf War-related illnesses resonate with the theme of *medical uncertainties.* Since the U.S. Army had denied using weapons containing DU or dioxins, the medical doctors at the V.A. hospitals were uncertain about the ill veterans' medical symptoms. Philips' article explained why the V.A. doctors were not certain whether the symptoms they could not identify were due to uranium or another type of dioxin.

Bill Mesler's (*The Nation,* May 26, 1997) article illustrated the insidious action of DU in the human body by scientists at the Defense Department Armed Forces Radiobiology Research Institute in Maryland. Mesler wrote,

> The American Association for Cancer Research (AACR) and Society of Toxicology tested the effects of embedded depleted uranium by inserting shrapnel-like pellets into the legs of rats, and they were surprised at how quickly they discovered oncogenes believed to be precursors to cancer. Another finding by the AARC was that depleted uranium kills suppressor, or health-maintaining, genes.

The AACR's toxicological finding resonates with the themes of *unexplained physical symptoms* and *long lasting unexplained physical symptoms.* In his testimony before the Congressional Sub-Committee on Human Resources, a Committee for Government Reform and Oversight (U. S. House of Representatives, June 26, 1997), Dr. Durakovic estimated that 123,000 troops had been exposed to depleted uranium through contact with captured Iraqi tanks. When asked by the sub-committee about the assessment of the troops who had been exposed to depleted uranium in the Gulf, he said,

The Human & Environmental cost of Wars

all work that was conducted on behalf of depleted uranium contamination was coordinated through the Persian Gulf Registry of the Wilmington VA hospital and all records were subsequently lost.

Bernstein, Dennis, and Kelley wrote an article entitled, "The Gulf War and the spread of sickness" (*The Progressive,* Mar. 1995, pp. 30-34). Their article claimed that the United States and Canada were not the only two countries where Gulf veterans were reporting health problems. They wrote,

> Dr. Saleh Al-Harbi at the Kuwait Ministry of Public Health has verified that a significant number of Kuwaiti citizens are suffering from a variety of chronic illnesses evidently induced by exposure.

The U.S. Senate Sub-Committee on Banking, Housing, and Urban Affairs (May 25, 1994) held a hearing to investigate the health of Gulf War veterans. The hearing was held to address complaints from several Gulf War veterans from Michigan that the Department of Veteran's Affairs was not adequately treating their medical symptoms. Senator Riegle the chairman of the committee, told the other members of the committee that from the medical symptoms of which the Gulf War veterans were complaining, it appeared they were suffering from Gulf War Syndrome.

VA officials who testified during the hearing informed members of the committee that many of the Gulf War veterans who have complained about their illnesses were being treated symptomatically. The VA officials tried to convince the members in the committee that there were no long-lasting, positive effects on the health of the complaining Gulf War veterans. The denial by officials of the U.S. Department of Veterans Affairs of the existence of long-lasting health effects while many Gulf War veterans were being referred for

The Human & Environmental cost of Wars

psy -chiatric evaluation relates to the theme of *medical uncertainties.* The medical uncertainty of the VA officials illustrates the theme of *unresponsive medical system.*

The issues of chemical warfare agents had been brought to attention of the U.S. Senate Committee on Banking, Housing and Urban Affairs Chairman Senator Riegle as early as in July of 1993 when the then Czechoslovakia minister of defense announced that Czechoslovakia chemical decontamination units had detected that chemical warfare agent Sarin. Senator Riegle released a staff report on the Czechoslovakia defense minister's report in September 1993. This information became known to the public in a declassified document released by the U.S. Senate Committee on Banking, Housing and Urban Affairs.

The unclassified report released by the committee points to the themes of *environment and health consequences* and *contamination of the natural resources and the environment.* It was mentioned in the unclassified report that, "The United States Department of Veterans believes that tens of thousands of U. S. Gulf veterans are suffering from the symptoms associated with the Gulf War Syndrome" (U.S. Senate, Hearing, May 25, 1994).

Veterans who testified during the U. S. Senate Hearing reported an array of medical symptoms ranging from muscle and joint pain, memory loss, intestinal and heart problems, fatigue, nasal congestion, urinary urgency, diarrhea, twitching, rashes, sores, and a number of other symptoms. Their testimonies revealed that they began experiencing these multiple

The Human & Environmental cost of Wars

symptoms during and after their tour of duty, and their symptoms often continued many months after their tour of duty.

The claims of the veterans who testified during the Senate hearings were supported by Chairman Riegle. Furthermore, Riegle (U.S. Senate Hearing, May 25, 1994 p. 2) told the other members of the committee that in virtually every case, the Gulf War veterans were in excellent physical condition when they went to the Gulf. In fact, he said,

> Under the voluntary Army arrangements, you have to be in exceptionally good condition today just to qualify for service in the Armed Forces, and that was particularly true for many who were asked to serve in the Gulf War.

The U. S. Committee of Banking Housing and Urban Affairs unclassified report also cites an increasing number of cases of spouses and children who report the same symptoms as the veterans, indicating a strong possibility of the transmissibility of the condition. In her opening statement (U.S. Senate, Hearing, May 25, 1994, pp. 7-8)

Senator Barbara Boxer of California,

> Informed members of hundreds, if not thousands, of California veterans are now suffering from Gulf War Syndrome. Many of them have come into my office; they have told me of their lives disrupted and families destroyed

In addition, Senator Bond informed other members of the committee that thousands of American servicemen and women are suffering from symptoms and undiagnosed disorders. According to Senator Bond, "It is consistent with exposure to biological or chemical toxins. I think, collectively, the facts make it at least possible that these Gulf War veterans were exposed to chemical and/or biological toxins" (U.S. Senate, Hearing, May 25, 1994, p.12).

The Human & Environmental cost of Wars

In his opening statement to the committee Under Secretary of Defense for Personnel and Readiness, Edwin Dorn, testified that, contrary to reports in the press that some veterans were exposed to chemical or biological weapons agent, (U.S. Senate, Hearing, May 25, 1994, pp. 15-16).

> There is no information, classified or unclassified, that indicates that chemical or biological weapons were used in the Persian Gulf. We're especially concerned about those Desert Shield and Desert Storm veterans who since the war have developed symptoms whose causes we cannot identify. These veterans represent a small portion of the nearly 700,000 U.S. military personnel who served in the Persian Gulf region during the conflict, and indeed, they represent a small portion of those who have been treated for illnesses or injuries suffered during the war

In his testimony to the Senate Committee on the Health of Persian Gulf War veterans, Dr. John Kriese, Chief Officer for Ground Forces, Defense Intelligence Agency, testified that "no chemical or biological weapons were found in Kuwait theater operations, meaning those portions of southern Iraq and Kuwait that constituted the battlefield. We did not find any chemical or biological munitions, live or spent, among the thousands of tons of munitions recovered on the battlefield" (U.S. Senate, Hearing, May 25, 1994, pp. 18-19).

On September 19, 1996, during the 103rd Congress, the director of the Gulf War Research Foundation, James J. Tuite, III, appeared before the Committee on Government Reform Oversight U. S. House of Representatives to illustrate the way the issue of sick Gulf War veteran, was handled by the government. In his testimony, Tuite told the committee that the Gulf War veterans were suffering from Gulf War syndrome.

The Human & Environmental cost of Wars

Tuite informed the committee that administration officials and Department of Defense and Central Intelligence Agency bureaucrats since mid-1993 had been misleading Congress. In his testimony to the committee, Tuite broke ranks when he told them that "the facts continued to argue otherwise" (U. S. House of Representatives, September 19, 1996). Tuite informed the committee that the report he was submitting for inclusion into the record draws from the existence of documents of which he believed "gratuitously identified both vulnerabilities and intelligence methods and sources that were denied to Congress but given to international curiosity seekers by those in the Department of Defense responsible for protecting our soldiers" (U. S. House of Representatives, Sept. 19, 1996).

Tuite also testified to the House of Representative Governmental Reform and Oversight Committee that "a published peer-reviewed study by Dr. Goran Jamal of British veterans revealed that 14 of 14 randomly selected veterans all showed signs of peripheral neuron-pathies similar to those seen in victims of chronic organophosphate pesticide exposures" (U. S. House of Representatives, Sept. 19, 1996). Tuite concluded his testimony by informing the committee members that while his testimony "does not establish the link between low-level organo-phosphate chemical nerve agent exposure and Gulf War Syndrome, and that the exact processes responsible have not been identified it does, however, scientifically overturn the long-held government position that the troops were not exposed to chemical warfare agents in, as the Central Intelligence Agency Director Deutch claimed on CBS's 60 Minutes" (U. S. House of Representatives, Sept. 19, 1996).

The Human & Environmental cost of Wars

5.2. Summary: Analysis and Themes

The newspaper and magazine articles, reports from the electronic news media, and Congressional committee hearings, that this study of depleted uranium munitions examined, tell us that since the end of the first Gulf War, a large proportion of the veterans who served in the Persian Gulf region continue to experience chronic and often debilitating health conditions. Their health conditions have been characterized by numerous problems. Their health problems include severe and persistent headaches, cognitive problems, somatic pain, fatigue, respiratory conditions, gastrointestinal difficulties, and a vast array of other symptoms that doctors find difficult to diagnose.

There are numerous bodies of evidence from the newspaper and magazine reports to indicate that many of the veterans, if not all the veterans who served in the Persian Gulf War, were exposed to some kind of toxic substances. These sources provided insights into the conditions affecting not only the Gulf War veterans, but also the families of the Gulf War veterans, and the thousands, if not hundreds of thousands, of the civilians in the Persian Gulf region. This research suggests that the health conditions affecting these diverse groups of people appear to be complex.

The findings of this study can be summarized on the following observations. First, because of constant denials after the first Gulf War by civilian and military administrators in the U.S. Department of Defense that the military used weapons containing depleted uranium or chemical weapons, the medical community became baffled by what was happening

The Human & Environmental cost of Wars

to the veterans of the Gulf War. They failed to arrive at any medical explanation for the veterans' illnesses.

Second, Gulf War veterans interpreted this medical uncertainty as medical unresponsiveness. They felt let down and betrayed by their military commanders and their government for not knowing a cure for their symptoms. This apparent failure by the medical community to provide diagnostic legitimacy to the sufferers created impediments for timely medical solutions. As a result, the complaints of veterans and their families who were suffering from what later became known as Gulf War Related Illnesses (GWRI) were not well received by the general public, and funding for treatment was diminished.

Third, evidence from the hearing of the United States Senate Committee on Banking, Housing, and Urban Affairs on the health of Gulf War veterans suggested that the Department of Veterans Affairs was adequately treating the veterans' myriad of medical symptoms. Furthermore, the military establishment and the Pentagon continue to deny to the veterans and the American public that chemical or biological weapons were used during the Gulf War. The question that remains to be answered is this: What then was causing the strange symptoms to the Gulf War veterans and their families?

Finally, there is no explanation to explain the long-lasting adverse health effects and environmental pollution in Bosnia and Herzegovina and in the battlefield areas of the Persian Gulf regions that is convincing enough short of the admission that the weapons used during these military conflicts contained depleted uranium and other toxic substances. Findings suggest that the only medical and scientific explanations for such results are associated with exposure to hazardous materials.

Nothing short of munitions containing depleted uranium can explain the lingering health concerns and birth defects reported by Gulf War veterans and civilians in the Gulf areas. From the large body of evidence demonstrating excess morbidity in Gulf War veterans, this study has reached the objective conclusion that those service men and women who were deployed in the Persian Gulf regions have been affected by an abnormally high rate of chronic multi-symptom illnesses as a result to depleted uranium exposure.

One of the limitations this exploratory study has encountered has to do with direct comparison between those veterans who were deployed to the Persian Gulf region and those who served elsewhere or simply stayed in the United States. Many of the findings in other studies on undiagnosed conditions have reported significantly higher rates of illness among Gulf War veterans than non-deployed veterans. Many studies have documented prevalence estimates of multi-symptom illness in Gulf War veterans and non-Gulf War veterans. Other studies have suggested exposures to alternative contaminants as possibility. Nonetheless, itcan be asserted that a substantial proportion of Gulf War veterans are ill with multi-symptom conditions not explained by wartime stress or psychiatric illness.

From the array of evidence presented in this study, it is clear that service men and women who served a tour of duty in the Persian Gulf during Operations Desert Shield and Desert Storm have experienced significantly more chronic and often debilitating symptoms,

The Human & Environmental cost of Wars

illnesses, and undiagnosed conditions than veterans who were not deployed to that region. Growing bodies of medical and scientific research have indicated that an important component of the Gulf War veterans' illnesses is neurological in character.

Those who maintain that this explains the many war-related syndromes reported by servicemen assert that servicemen often experience unexplained symptoms after deployment to hostile areas. They view stress as an element common to all deployments, defining it as the extreme psychological trauma associated with a war zone. Despite the numerous Congressional reports and special government and scientific review panels, the controversy and challenges of understanding Gulf War veterans' illnesses remains elusive.

In summary, this chapter presented analysis and themes that emerged from newspaper and magazines articles, reports from the electronic news media, and document materials and electronic reports of Congressional committee hearings. The next chapter presents a discussion of possible mitigation strategies that, if employed, could ameliorate the damage associated with the use of depleted uranium munitions on the battlefield.

CHAPTER 6

MITIGATION OF THE EFFECTS OF DEPLETED URANIUM

The human health risks and the environmental hazards of the use of weapons containing depleted uranium in battlefields in three major military conflicts in Eastern Europe and the Middle East have become a much debated issue. It has been difficult to come to any significant conclusions to this debate since there has been very little scientific fieldwork with proper measurements as well as laboratory work done outside of the military community. Research studies conducted since the first Gulf War have consistently indicated that psychiatric illness, combat experience, or other deployment-related stressors do not explain Gulf War veterans' illnesses in the large majority of ill veterans.

Various documentary materials in newspaper and magazine articles, together with internet reports of testimonials presented in Congressional hearings by ill Gulf War veterans and their family members, have indicated that exposure to depleted uranium and other potentially toxic substances pose a risk to human health. Despite the breakthroughs in recent impressive research by the U.S. Department of Defense (USDOD), overall, these research efforts have not succeeded in answering the fundamental questions about what caused the Gulf War veterans' illnesses.

The Human & Environmental cost of Wars

All the Congressional reports, special government panels, and scientific review committees appointed to consider the effects of the use of munitions containing depleted uranium have unanimously acknowledged the seriousness of the problem. They have found evidence for both human life concerns and environmental degradation. But there has been no consensus when it comes to banning depleted uranium completely from military arsenals. Although scientific evidence linking depleted uranium use in battlefield to the undiagnosed symptoms of the Gulf War veterans is not conclusive, nonetheless, sufficient evidence exist from the literature to suggest that depleted uranium poses a threat to human health and the environment. How else are we to explain the undiagnosed symptoms reported by more than 250,000 deployed Gulf War veterans from the Persian Gulf, if not exposure to depleted uranium that USDOD has lately admitted using during the war?

If depleted uranium does not pose any danger to human life or the environment as military researchers are claiming, what then is responsible for the mysterious deaths of more than 8,000 of the veterans since the war ended more than a decade ago? How does the USDOD explain the 697,000 veterans of the Gulf War who have filed claims for veterans benefit based on service-related injuries and illnesses? How else does the USDOD explain the granting of over 159,000 veterans' disability payments if not as a result of exposure to depleted uranium during combat?

How else can the USDOD and those scientists who refused to link depleted uranium to human health risk and environmental hazards explain the more than 1.5 million soldiers and civilians in Iraq who have died of unnatural causes since 1991? How do they explain

The Human & Environmental cost of Wars

the increase at an alarming rate of leukemia, cancer, birth defects, and rare diseases of one-third of children under the age of 5 in Iraq and elsewhere in the Persian Gulf countries since 1991, the beginning of the First Gulf War?

There is convincing epidemiological and scientific evidence to indicate a causal relationship between depleted uranium exposure and many of the strange and undiagnosed illnesses Gulf War veterans and civilian populations in the Gulf area are experiencing many years after the end of the Gulf War even if scientific evidence presented by paid military scientists have dissociated any link between depleted uranium and human health. In addition to presenting a radiation hazard, depleted uranium is also a highly toxic substance. As with most heavy metals, it can disrupt the normal operation of many proteins that are essential for normal body functioning. For example, uranium's interference with renal proteins kidneys has been known for many years and has been widely documented. The United Nations Sub-commission on Human Rights, in its 1996 session, condemned weaponry containing depleted uranium as a weapon of mass destruction and its indiscriminate use against members of the armed forces and civilian populations. The Sub- commission spoke of these weapons not only as resulting in death, misery, and disability, but also as being incompatible with existing norms.

The Sub-commission was also concerned about the long-term consequences on human life and the environment following the use of depleted uranium on the battlefield.

The Human & Environmental cost of Wars

In a 1996 advisory opinion, the International Court of Justice (ICJ) affirmed that under humanitarian law, "States must never use weapons that are incapable of distinguishing between civilian and military targets" (ICJ 1996). The use of weapons containing depleted uranium violates humanitarian law, which prohibits indiscriminate or willful killing.

In each of the four Geneva Conventions, willful killing is a war crime under the great breach articles. Articles 51 and 52 of the Geneva Convention prohibits targeting civilian population or engaging in military operations likely to have indiscriminate and undue effect on the civilian population. Article 85 of the Geneva Convention makes any violations of article 51 and 52 grave breaches as war crimes. The controversy over depleted uranium use pits military interests against the health of citizens and soldiers around the world. The use of depleted uranium weapons places an unacceptable and excessive risk on human health and the environment.

As civilized nations of the world, it is in the interest of humanity and sanity of mankind that all nations should endeavor to stop the senseless tragedy, and pursue an international agreement to ban all weapons containing depleted uranium. As members of a civilized world community, nation states should collectively establish and enforce an International agreement that bans the military use of depleted uranium in all its forms, including its use in bombs, cruise missiles, munitions, and armor.

The international community should require all nations that are involved in the production, testing, and/or use of depleted uranium munitions to mitigate the environmental impact of their activities by conducting a full-scale and thorough cleanup of sites and battle-fields contaminated by their use of depleted uranium.

All governments should be encouraged to review their regulations and policies relating to the handling and disposal of radioactive waste materials and to establish appropriate cleanup procedures of sites contaminated with depleted uranium and other radioactive substances. These policies should include assurances that all personnel, whether civilian or military, working around depleted uranium be given adequate education and issue appropriate radiation protection to minimize possible health risks from radiation exposure. The international community should endeavor to embark on research to develop safe and effective cleanup methods for contaminated sites.

Nation states, as members of the international community, should come together in a joint effort to conduct independent health studies of Persian Gulf War veterans to determine the toxic and radiological effects of exposure to depleted uranium, and explain how these effects are distinct from Gulf War Syndrome. The soldiers and civilians, who were in locations where they could have been exposed to depleted uranium, should be thoroughly examined; for example, soldiers and civilians within a 25-mile radius of the depleted uranium ammunition fire in Doha, Kuwait should have urine analysis and in vivo whole-body gamma counting tests for depleted uranium.

Disaster researcher Fritz (1961), views disaster as an event that is concentrated in time and space, in which a society or relatively self-sufficient subdivision of society, under

The Human & Environmental cost of Wars

goes severe danger, and incurs such loses to its members and physical that the social structure is disrupted and the fulfillment of all or some of the essential function of the society is prevented. Similarly Quarantelli (1998) another disaster researcher views disaster as a catastrophic situation by which normal life is severely disrupted.

The human-hazard interaction perspective of a disaster is seen by some disaster researchers Mileti (1999), Mitchell and Thomas (2002), and White (1974) as providing a useful framework to understand the dynamic mechanisms of disasters. This perspective views natural disasters as a conflict between the earth's physical system and the human use system, which can be moderated by hazard adjustments. As seen from the human-hazard interaction perspective a disaster occurs when extreme natural events trigger chain impacts. The chain impacts whether direct or indirect, is seen as causing the primary physical impacts on constructed physical environments such as residential buildings and critical facilities as well as directly generating human casualties.

The term mitigation applies to a wide range of activities and protection measures that might be instigated, from the physical, like constructing stronger buildings, to the procedural, like standard techniques for incorporating hazard assessment in land-use planning. Disaster mitigation is the term used to refer to all actions to reduce the impact of a disaster that can be taken prior to occurrence, including preparedness and long-term risk reduction measures. It includes both planning and implementation of measures to reduce the risks associated with known natural and human-made hazards, and the process of planning for effective response to disasters which occur.

The Human & Environmental cost of Wars

Mitigation reduces and limits the destructive and disruptive effects of hazards on the elements at risk. Measures range from the physical such as engineering works like bridges, protective dikes, embankments, and safe building design to the non-structural intervention such as community risk assessment, community risk reduction planning, public awareness, crop insurance, strengthening community disaster management organizations and advocacy on disasters and development issues, legislation and land use zoning. Disaster research scholars Twigg et al (2002), believes that mitigation and prevention interventions are directly linked to development planning. These disaster researchers believe that disaster mitigation is an intrinsic part of sustainable development. Mitigation involves not only saving lives and injury and reducing property losses, but also reducing the adverse consequences of natural hazards to economic activities and social institutions.

Mitigation means taking actions to reduce the effects of a hazard before it occurs. The aim of mitigation strategy is to reduce losses in the event of a future occurrence of a hazard. The primary aim is to reduce the risk of death and injury to the population. The Secondary aim include reducing damage and economic losses inflicted on public sector infrastructure and reducing private sector losses in as far likely to include encouragement for people to protect themselves as far as possible. Any mitigation strategy is likely to include a range of measures, a set of actions that includes some engineering measures, some spatial planning, and a degree of economic management and societal inputs. A mitigation strategy has to be designed for its proposed applications.

The Human & Environmental cost of Wars

Successful mitigation strategy has to be designed for its proposed application. Successful mitigation entails a number of fundamental changes in the attitudes of the people at risk, in the processes of creating and modifying the physical environment and the physical layout of the community. Mitigation strategies will in many cases be incorporated as an element of larger scale development programs; any successful strategy should include a range of measures from the menu of possible actions. A disaster mitigation effort is an attempt to prevent hazards from developing into disasters altogether or to reduce the effects of disasters when they occur. The need for emergency management personnel to take a more holistic view to mitigate against hazards, such as depleted uranium and other substances hazardous to human health and the environment, has been demonstrated in the medical and scientific research findings in this study. Depleted uranium and toxic substances mitigation will only occur when there is consensus among nation states with stockpiles of depleted uranium in their military arsenals that such a holistic disaster emergency management approach is desirable, feasible, and affordable.

George and Bullock (2003) explained in their publication "Introduction to Emergency Management," that the mitigation phase differs from other phases because it focuses on long-term measures for reducing or eliminating risk. They indicate that the implementation of mitigation strategies should be considered a part of the disaster recovery process if applied after a disaster occurs. The aim of emergency management mitigation planning for depleted uranium and other toxic substances should be to develop a disaster safety culture in which people are fully aware of the hazards they face when exposed to depleted uranium and other toxic substances, to help protect them as fully as they can, and to fully support efforts on their behalf to protect them.

A holistic approach will help protect human health and the environment against future technological hazards, such as depleted uranium and other toxic substances. Many developing nation states face enormous resource constraints in addressing disaster risk. Their scarce resources constrain them from shifting their priorities from regular urban management and development to disaster mitigation. Regular decisions about planning, staffing, and budgeting can reflect disaster reduction priorities effectively, if the nation's emergency management personnel has a mitigation strategy and a plan for its implementation.

Emergency management personnel can increase public awareness about the dangers of disaster hazards by implementing new public policy and public infrastructure. Private firms should include mitigation procedures as part of their regulatory processes. Disaster reduction can be achieved by investing monies as part of new construction costs. Mitigation planning should be used to promote a risk-based approach to development in which sustainable development is based on an understanding and management of all risks: environmental, physical, economic, and social.

A nation's community development best practices should involve emergency disaster preparedness project that will work in that community. Depleted uranium and technological toxin substance disaster prevention and mitigation programs should incorporate networking initiatives into the designs, whereby, communities become linked to

The Human & Environmental cost of Wars

government and non-government agencies that can provide financial resources for higher-end, more material-intensive solutions.

There is a growing awareness that emergency management disaster mitigations operations are more complex and comprehensive than traditionally perceived. There is a realization among emergency management personnel that their primary function in every disaster mitigations involving technological hazards, such as depleted uranium and other technological chemical substances, is to protect human life, property, and the environment. This awareness involves not just crisis-reactive responses to emergencies, but also finding ways to avoid problems in the first place and preparing for those that will undoubtedly occur. This inclusive approach to emergency management can be considered as occurring in four stages: pre-disaster mitigation and prevention, pre-disaster preparedness, disaster response, and post-disaster response to recovery.

Quarantelli (1997) suggested that a successful disaster emergency management is a cyclical activity which includes five stages: a) pre-disaster preventive mitigating actions; b) the-formation of emergency plans and preparedness activities; c) emergency disaster relief interventions; d) short-term recovery and rehabilitation; and e) long-term reconstruction. In the preparedness phase, emergency management personnel should develop plans of action for when the disaster strikes. Measures taken by emergency managers in the pre-disaster phase should include the proper maintenance and training of emergency services, and develop and exercise emergency population warning measures combined with evacuation plans.

The Human & Environmental cost of Wars

The formation of emergency plans and preparedness activities should involve the development and integration of multi-agency coordination by emergency management personnel as an efficient preparedness measure. First, emergency management personnel must implement steps that must follow emergency assessment before exposure reduction procedures can occur. The emergency assessment procedure must include warnings that must be disseminated to the risk area population. As Mileti and Peek (2000) indicate, at the initial stage of a catastrophic disaster or disasters in general emergency management, personnel must make sure the risk area populations are the first people to receive the warning, understand it, accept it, and prepare to take protective action.

Agency integration efforts must act as an efficient preparedness measure in case of any disaster emergencies, but only when steps have been taken by emergency management personnel to protect the risk area can they be certain to have accomplished disaster exposure reduction or avoidance. Alexander (2002) indicates the emergency disaster relief intervention phase is the response stage. During the response stage, emergency management personnel should include the mobilization of the necessary emergency services and first responders, such as firefighters, police, volunteers, and non-governmental organizations, such as the Red Cross, in the disaster area. Emergency management personnel should coordinate a well rehearsed disaster emergency plan as part of the preparedness phase to enable them to execute an efficient coordination of rescue efforts.

The Human & Environmental cost of Wars

The aim of the recovery phase as indicated by Alexander is to restore the affected area to its previous state. Emergency management personnel's main focus during this phase should be with issues and decisions that should be made after immediate needs are addressed. George and Bullock (2004) state that emergency management personnel, during the recovery efforts, should be concerned with actions that involve rebuilding destroyed property, re-employment, and repair of other essential infrastructure.

Quarantelli's (1997) five disaster mitigating stages must integrate research and development, information exchange, capacity building and training, and implementation of appropriate solutions to vulnerable communities in order to be effective. From an emergency management perspective, these various stages of disaster reduction can easily be managed by through the following methods: specialized fellowships and producing specialized technical publications for researchers, policy makers, and the public on such issues as hazard mapping, risk and vulnerability assessment, legal and economic aspects of disaster reduction, and the use of economic and fiscal incentives for disaster reduction purposes; organizing regional, sub-regional, national, and local workshops and seminars for residents in the community, researchers, and government officials; and developing strategies, programs, and project for efficient disaster reduction in specific circumstances in response to official national requests.

To reduce the impact disasters have on built-in communities and to protect human lives and property, emergency management personnel should advocate for improved policies for disaster reduction by working with other parts of the United Nations organizations,

The Human & Environmental cost of Wars

national and local governments, the research and development community, the private business sectors, and non-governmental organizations (NGOs). Although there are various industries and fields of activity often in place to deal with safety regulations to prevent the occurrence or reduce the effects of technological disasters, such as depleted uranium, when systems fail or are inadequate the results can be catastrophic.

The lessons from Three Mile Island (TMI) and Chernobyl have taught us that to prevent future technological disaster occurrences in the magnitude of those two disasters; we have to first and foremost restructure our national policy on disaster management to reflect the holistic approach. This would entail implementation of policies to insure prevention, mitigation, and preparedness in pre-disaster planning with appropriate funding.

The existing emergency management frameworks focus primarily on post-disaster relief and rehabilitation under crisis management. For an emergency management program to be implemented effectively during a technological disaster, such as depleted uranium or any catastrophic events, appropriate amendments should be introduced in the legislative and regulatory instruments of nation states. In addition, enforcement mechanisms must be strengthened at different levels. The capacity building for effective disaster management should start at the local and regional levels for undertaking rapid assessment surveys and investigations of the nature and extent of damage in post disaster situations.

The creative efforts, for example, of the United Nations in the aftermath of the Chernobyl disaster were naturally targeted to meet the wide-scale humanitarian needs.

The Human & Environmental cost of Wars

Twenty years after Chernobyl, the legacy still remains strong. The effects of radioactive contamination are still being felt in the affected regions. In the Chernobyl disaster, more than 59,000 square kilometers, covering 14 regions of the Russian federation, were contaminated. In Iraq and throughout the Gulf region, evidence suggests that some bombing sites were contaminated by bombs containing depleted uranium. From an emergency management perspective, it is recommended that any loose contamination, such as penetrators and fragments, should be picked up only by authorized personnel.

Emergency management personnel should inform military personnel and those who have been assigned to mine clearance about the proper procedures for handling bomb fragments and of the risks associated with depleted uranium. The UNEP assessment team, working in collaboration with emergency management personnel, should recommend to field investigators the equipment that is appropriate for making complementary searches for possible local ground contamination of significance; and for detecting the presence of penetrators, jackets and casings, and contamination points on the ground surface.

A UNEP environmental assessment finding also suggests the feasibility of any necessary clean-up and decontamination measures assessed. The risk of depleted uranium dispersion in air and inhalation should be considered before planning for any soil disturbance or removal of vegetation. It is suggested by UNEP that an appropriate contingency plan should be developed prior to ground-breaking activities when working at sites were DU weapons had been used.

The UNEP environmental assessment team also suggests that the responsible authorities should develop a training course of designated personnel to act as authorized persons in the field of depleted uranium mitigation. Clean-up measures would ideally be included in such a course. It is also suggested that the relevant health authorities should continue the development of a cancer reporting system and registry, and investigate claims of health effects from exposure to depleted uranium in order to determine any increased incidences of health issues.

To summarize, this chapter has presented a discussion for mitigating depleted uranium from an emergency management personnel perspective. Emergency management personnel must understand the risk population perceptions of hazards, be able to provide the public with credible information about the ensuing dangers, and correct any public misperceptions about it. Minimizing the chance of unnecessary depleted uranium's exposure requires emergency management personnel taking action as early as possible to decrease the likelihood of unnecessary danger to the risk population and the environment.

In conclusion, this study on Mitigation of Human Health and the Environment has presented evidence from medical and scientific studies indicating that depleted uranium munitions on the battlefield are hazardous to human health and the environment. Even though there are contradictions in many of the scientific and medical findings about human health effects and environmental hazards from the use of depleted uranium, this exploratory study has provided the assessment of the implications and dangers of toxic substances on

The Human & Environmental cost of Wars

human health and its environmental consequences, and has demonstrated the urgency to find ways to mitigate its use in weapons in military conflicts, and to eventually ban it from battlefields. This study has discussed the etiological role of depleted uranium in the genesis of Gulf War-related illnesses by highlighting some of the medical and scientific studies that show the human health risks and the environmental hazards caused by the use of such weapons.

In keeping with the principles of grounded theory as practiced by Glass and Straus (1967), this study assessed the data and analysis collected from newspapers, magazines, and electronic media reports. Through a process of theoretical sampling, I was able to analyze information from the document materials that were directed by the emerging theory. The thematic analysis that evolves during the collection of the document materials, such as medical uncertainties, unresponsive medical systems, unexplained physical symptoms, and long-lasting unexplained physical symptoms emerges from electronic media reports of Gulf War veteran's testimonies before U.S. Congressional Committee hearings, and from newspaper interviews and reports of the medical conditions of the sick veterans.

The thematic analysis provided a fresh slant from materials that were collected from newspapers, magazines, and electronic media reports. The application and use of an intensive analytical process made it possible to analyze information from the document materials. This analytic process was driven by the emerging theory through the process of theoretical sampling. The emerging theory was controlled by the process of data collection. The data that was extracted from the document materials were directed by the emerging

The Human & Environmental cost of Wars

theory. Through a process of a constant comparative method, significant statements were extracted from the document materials, coded and grouped thematically, and were used in organizing the data within broad themes. I looked for emerging patterns and themes from the data by exploring the differences and similarities across incidents within the data collected from the document materials.

This method provides the guidelines for collecting additional data. The theoretical framework in this study is social constructionism, a sociological approach articulated by Luckman & Berger (1966), which recognizes social involvement within a social context for meaning gained through retrospective and emergent contexts. The theory of social constructionism is used for explaining how Gulf War veterans and their families perceive and interpret the meanings of their illnesses that grew out of their experiences within weaponry under battlefield conditions. Future research that focuses on other phenomenon which appears to be related to exposure of toxic and other biological chemicals on vulnerable non-combatants is needed

The Human & Environmental cost of Wars

Photo reproduced courtesy
The remains of an Iraqi tank abandoned in the demilitarized zone near Kuwaiti border. The two holes in the side of the tank were made by depleted uranium penetrators.

The Human & Environmental cost of Wars

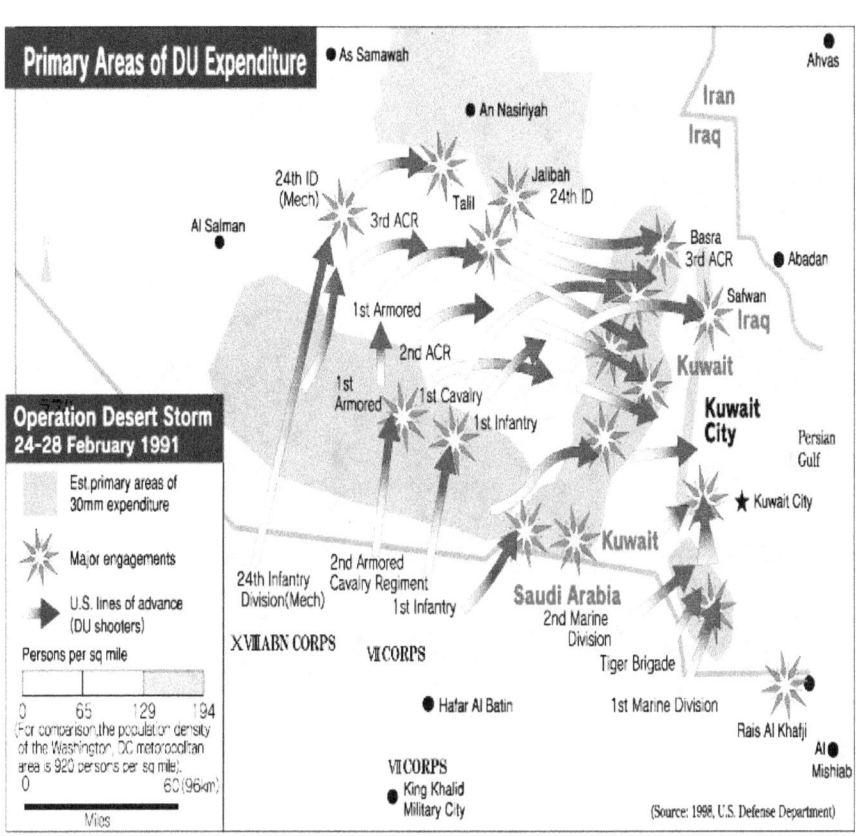

Map of primary areas DU Expenditure reproduced courtesy of the U.S. Defense Department (DOD, 1998).

The Human & Environmental cost of Wars

Photo courtesy of Douglas Rokke.
U.S. soldiers investigating radioactive contamination and potential protective measures after firing DU shells at an Iraqi tank. The soldiers in the photo are wearing protective clothing and masks to prevent contamination. (Taken June 1995, at the nuclear test site in Nevada)

The Human & Environmental cost of Wars

The Human & Environmental cost of Wars

REFERENCES

ABC News Nightline, Ted Koppel interview with Betty Mekdeci, Dec. 27, 1995.

AEPI, U.S. Army Environmental Policy Institute. (1995). "Health and Environmental Consequences of Depleted Uranium use in the U.S. Army," June 1995, 154.
American Sociological Review, Vol. 16, No. 6, 812-818.

Arfsten, D. P., Still K. R., & Ritchie, G. D. (2001). A review of the effects of uranium and
depleted uranium exposure on reproduction and fetal development. *Toxicology and
Industrial Health*. 17: 180-191.

Associated Press, August 12, 2006, free archived copy at:
http://www.commondreams.org/headlines06/0812-06.htm
\
Baltimore Sun, February 4, 2001.

Berger, Peter, L. & Luckman, Thomas (1966). *The Social Construction of Reality: A Treatise in the Sociology of Knowledge*. New York: Anchor Books/Doubleday.

Bernstein, D. & K. The Gulf War and the Spread of Sickness. *The Progressive*, March
1995, 30-34.

Brown, P. (1999). *The Guardian* Oct. 27, 1999.

Brown, P., et al. (2001). A Gulf of Difference: Disputes over Gulf War-Related Illnesses.
Journal of Health and Social Behavior, Vol. 42, No. 3, 235-257.

Bullock, Jane A., & George Bullock. (2003). *Introduction to Emergency Management*. Bur-
lington, MA: Butterworth-Heinemann.

Centers for Disease Control and Prevention. (1995). Unexplained illness among Persian
Gulf War veterans in an Air National Guard Unit: Preliminary report, August 1990-
March 1995. *Journal of American Medical Association*. 1995, 274:167.

Charatan, F. (2002). U.S links motor neurone disease with Gulf war service.
British Medical Journal. 2002; 324:65.

The Human & Environmental cost of Wars

Clark, R. (1999). Control of low-level radiation exposure: Time for change? *Journal of Radiological Protection. 19(2), 107-115*

Cohen, N. (1991) Radioactive Waste Left in Gulf by Allies. *The Independent, Britain*, No. 94, November 10, 1991.

Cohen, S. T. (1978). Enhanced Radiation Warheads: Setting the Record Straight. *Strategic Review*, Winter 1978, p. 10.

Cross, Major Thomas (1996). *Status of Efforts to Identify Persian Gulf War Syndrome.* 104th Cong., 2d session, Human Resources and Intergovernmental Relations Subcommittee hearings, p. 48, Nos. 1-4.

Durakovic, A. (1999). Medical effects of internal contamination with uranium. *Croatian Medical Journal, 1999, 40:49-66.*

Durakovic, A. (2003). Undiagnosed Illnesses and Radioactive Warfare. *Croatian Medical Journal*, 44(5), 520-532.

Durakovic, A., Horan, P., Dietz, L. A & Zimmerman, I. (2003). Estimate of the time zero lung burden of depleted uranium in Persian Gulf War veterans by the 24-hour urinary excretion and exponential decay analysis. *Mil Med*, 2003, 168:600-605.

Fahey, D. (1998). Case Narrative: Depleted Uranium Exposures. Swords to Plowshares, National Gulf war Resource Center, the Military Toxics Project. 3rd ed., September 20, 1998.

Fetter, S., & Von Hippel F. (1999). The hazard posed by depleted-uranium munitions. *Science and Global Security*, 1999, 8(2).

Flanders, L. Mal de guerre (1994). *The Nation*. March 7, 1994:292-293.

Flanders, L. (1995) A Lingering Sickness. *The Nation*, January 23, 1995:94, 96.

Fritz, C.E. (1961). "Disaster." In R.K. Merton & R.A. Nisbet (Eds.), *Contemporary Social Problems*, 651-694, New York: Harcourt.

Fujikiwa, Y., Shizuma, K., Endo, S., Fukui, M., Anomalous. (2003). $_{235}U/_{238}U$ ratios and metal elements detected in the black rain from the Hiroshima A-bomb. *Journal of the Health Physics Society*, 2003, 84:155-162.

The Human & Environmental cost of Wars

Fukuda, K., Nisenbaum, R., Stewart, G., Thompson, W.W., Robin, L., Washko, R.M., Noah, D.L., Barrett, D.H., Randall, B., Herwaldt, B.L., Mawle, A.C., & Reeves, W.C. (1998). Chronic multisymptom illness affecting Air Force veterans of the Gulf War. *Journal of the American Medical Association,* 1998, 280(11):981-988.

Goss Gilroy Inc. (1998). *Health Study of Canadian Forces Personnel Involved in the 1991 Conflict in the Persian Gulf.* Canadian epidemiological study of Gulf War Veterans. Vol. 1. Ottawa, Ontario.

Goss Gilroy Inc. Prepared for the Department of National Defense. http://www.DND.ca/menu/press/reports/health/healthGoss Gilroy Inc.

Glaser, Barney G., & Straus, Anselm L. (1967). *The Discovery of Grounded Theory: Strategies for Qualitative Research.* New York: Aldine Publishing Company.

Gray, G.C., Coate, B.D., Anderson, C.M., Kang, H.K., Berg, S.W., Wignall, F.S., Knoke, J.D & Barrett-Connor, E. (1996). The postwar hospitalization experience of US Persian Gulf War Veterans. *New England Journal of Medicine,* 1996, 335:1505-1513.

Gray, G.C., Kaiser, K.S., Hawksworth, A.W., Hall, F.W., & Barrett-Connor, E.L. (1999). Increased postwar symptoms and psychological morbidity among US Navy Gulf War veterans. *Amer J Trop Med Hyg,* 1999, 60:758-766.

Gray, G.C., Smith, T.C., Knoke, J.D., & Heller, J.M. (1999) The postwar hospitalization experience of Gulf War veterans possibly exposed to chemical munitions destruction at Khamisiyah, Iraq. *American Journal of Epidemiology,* 1999, 150:532-540.

Gu, G., Zhu, S., Wang, L., & Yang, S. (2002). Irradiation of 235 uranium growth, behavior and some biochemical changes of brain in neonatal rats [in Chinese]. *Wei Sheng Yan Jiu,* 2001, 30:257-259.

Gulf War Illness Advisory Committee, Department of National Defense. (1998). Health *study of Canadian Forces Personnel Involved in the 1991 Conflict in the Persian Gulf.* Volume 1, Ottawa, Ontario: Goss Gilroy, Inc.

Haley R.W. & Kurt T.L. (1999). Self-reported exposure to neurotoxic chemical combinations in the Gulf War: a cross-sectional epidemiologic study. *Journal of American Medical association,* 1997, 277:231-237.

Haley, R.W., Hom, J., & Roland P.S. (1997). Evaluation of Neurologic Function in Gulf War Veterans: A Blinded Case-Control Study. *Journal of the American Medical Association,* 277:223-230.

The Human & Environmental cost of Wars

Hedges, C. (1999). *New York Times,* July 14, 1999

Holley, D. (1999) U. N. urges cleanup of 'Hotspots' left by Kosovo War. *The New York Times* October 27, 1999.

Hooper, F.J., Squibb, K.S., Siegle, E.L., McPhaul, K., & Keogh, J.P. (1999). Elevated urine uranium excretion by soldiers with retained uranium shrapnel. *Journal of Health Physics Society* 1999, 77(5):512-519.

Horan, P., Dietz, L., & Durakovic, A. (2002). "The quantitative analysis of depleted uranium isotopes in British, Canadian, and U.S. Gulf War veterans." *Mil. Med,* 167:620–27.

Independent on Sunday, Nov. 10, 1991.

Institute Of Medicine of the National Academies (2005). Mortality in US Army Gulf War Veterans Exposed to 1991 Khamisiyah Chemicals Munitions Destruction.

Johnson, L. (2003). Lingering health concerns and birth defects. *The Seattle Post Intelligencer*, August 4, 2003.

Jones, H. (1999) *New York Times*, November 22, 1999.

Kang, H.K., & Bullman, T.A. (1996). Mortality among U.S. veterans of the Persian Gulf War. *New England Journal of Medicine,* 1996, 335(20):1498-1504.

Kang, H.K., & Bullman, T. A. (2000). Illness among United States Veterans of the Gulf War: A Population-Based Survey of 30,000 Veterans. *Journal of Occupational and Environmental Medicine,* May 2000, 42(5):491-500.

Kang, Han; Magee, Carol; Mahan, Clare; Lee, Kyung; Murphy, Frances; Jackson, Leila; & Mantanoski, Genevieve (2001). Pregnancy Outcomes Among U.S. Gulf War Veterans: A Population-Based Survey of 30,000 Veterans. *Ann. Epidemiol,* 11:504–511.

Kang, HK, & Bullman, T.A. (1996) Mortality among U.S. veterans of the Persian Gulf War. *New England Journal of Medicine*, 335(20):1498-1504.

Kang, HK, & Bullman, T.A. (2001). Mortality among U.S. veterans of the Persian Gulf War: 7 year follow-up. *Journal of Epidemiology*, Vol. 154, No. 5, pp.399-405.

The Human & Environmental cost of Wars

Kang H.K., Natelson B.H., Mahan C.M., Lee, K.Y., & Murphy F.M. (2003). Post-traumatic stress disorder and chronic fatigue syndrome-like illness among Gulf War veterans: A population-based survey of 30,000 veterans. *American Journal of Epidemiology,* 2003, 157:141-148.

Kennedy, Bruce P., Ichiro Kawachi, & Deborah Prothrow-Smith. (1996). Income distribution and mortality: cross sectional ecological study of the Robin Hood index in the United States. *BMJ,* April 20, 1996, 312:1004-1007.

Kirby, A. (2002) *The Guardian, March* 22, 2000.

Leenhouts, H. P., Brugmans, M. J., & Bijwaard, H. (2002). The implications of re-analyzing radiation-induced leukemia in atomic bomb survivors: risk of acute and chronic exposures is different. *Journal of Radiological Protection,* 22: A, 163-167.
Los Angeles Times, Nov. 1994.

Laura, J. (1999). Effects of American and NATO bombs on human health and the environment. *The Globe,* Aug. 6, 1999.

Lubenau, J.O., & Strom, D. J. (2002). Safety and security of radiation sources in the aftermath of 11 September 2001. *Journal of Health Physics Society,* 83:155-164.

Little, M.P. (2002). The Proportion of thyroid cancers in the Japanese atomic bomb survivors associated with background radiation. *Journal of Radiological Protection,* 22:279-291.
Maconocchie, N., Doyle, P., Roman, E., Davies, G., Smith, P.G., & Beral, V. (1999). Nuclear industry family study: methods and description of a United Kingdom study linking occupational information held by employers to reproduction and child health. *Journal of the American College of Occupational and Environmental Medicine,* 1999, 56:798-808.

Maconocchie, N., Doyle, P. & Carson, C. (2004). Infertility among male UK veterans of the 1990-1 Gulf war: reproductive cohort study. *British Medical Journal,* 329, 196-201.

Marshall, G.M., Darvis, & L.M., Sherbourne C.D. (1999) A Review of the Scientific Literature as it Pertains to Gulf War Illnesses. *Vol 4: Stress*. Washington, D.C., RAND.

Marshall, Albert C. (2005). *An Analysis of Uranium Dispersal and Health Effects Using Gulf War Case Study*. National Security Studies Department Scandia National Laboratories. Washington, D.C.

The Human & Environmental cost of Wars

McDiarmid, M.A., Keogh, J. P., Hooper, F.J., McPhaul, K., Squibb, K., Kane, R., DiPino, R., Kabat, M., Kaup, B., Anderson, L., Hoover, D., Brown, L., Hamilton, M., Jacobson-Kram, D., Burrow, B., & Walsh, M. (2000). Health effects of depleted uranium on exposed Gulf War veterans. *Environmental Research,* 82(2):168-180.

Mettler, F.A. Jr., et al. (1999). *Potential Radiation Exposure in Military Operations, An Evaluation of Radiation Guidance for Military Operations.* Institute of Medicine, National Academy Press, Washington, DC, 23-24.

Miller, Briggs, & Hudson (1992). *Life Magazine,* July 1992.

Miller, R. L. (1986). *Under the cloud: the decades of nuclear testing.* New York: Free Press (Division of McMillan Inc.).

Miller, A., Blakely, W., Livengood, D., Whittaker, T., Jiaquan X., Ejnik, J., Hamilton, M., Parlette, E., St. John, T., Gerstenberg, H., & Hsu, H. (1998). Transformation of Human Osteoblast Cells to the Tumorigenic Phenotype by Depleted Uranium-Uranyl Chloride. *Environmental Health Perspectives* Volume 106 Number 8, August 1998.

Mesler, B. (1997). *The Nation,* May 26, 1997.

Mileti, D.S. (1999). *Disaster by design: A reassessment of Natural Hazards in the United States.* Washington, D.C: Joseph Henry Press.

Mitchell, J. T. & Thomas, D.S.K. (2002). *Trends in Disaster Losses. Chapter 5 in American Hazardscapes: The Regionalization of Hazards and Disasters.* Washington, DC: Joseph Henry Press.

Parkhurst, M. A., et al. (2004). Capstone Depleted Uranium Aerosols: Generation and Characterization, Volumes 1 and 2. PNNL-14168, Prepared for the United States Army by Pacific Northwest National Laboratory, Richland, Washington, October 2004.

Pellmar, T.C., Keyser, D.O., Emery, C., & Hogan, J.B. (1999b). Electrophysiological changes in hippocampal slices isolated from rats embedded with depleted uranium fragments. *Neurotoxicology,* 1999b, 20(5); 785-792.

Pierce, P. (1997). Physical and emotional health of Gulf War veteran women. *Aviation, Space, and Environmental Medicine.* 1997, 68:317-21.

Pierce, P., Antonakos, C., Deroba, B.A. (1999). Health care utilization and satisfaction

The Human & Environmental cost of Wars

concerning gender-specific health problems among military women. *Mil Med,* 1999, 164:98-102.

Philip, S. (1996). Studies seem to back veterans who trace illnesses to Gulf War. *The New York Times.* November 26, 1996.

Philip, S. (1996) *The New York Times,* Dec. 3, 1996

Plant, J. A., Kinniburg, D. G., Smedley, P. L., Fordice., Smedley, P. L., Fordyce, F. M., & Klink, B. A. (2004). Arsenic and s, 17-66. In: Lolar, B. S. (Ed), *Environmental Geochemistry,* vol. 9. In: Holland, H. D, and Turekian, K. K. (Eds), Treatise on Geochemistry, Elsevier-Pergamon, Oxford.

Presidential Advisory Committee (1996). *Gulf War Veteran's Illnesses: Final Report.* Washington, D.C.: US Government Printing Office, December 1996, published on Gulf LINK (http://www.gulflink.osd.mil).

Presidential Advisory Committee on Gulf War Veterans' Illnesses (1996a). *Interim Report.* Washington DC: U.S. Government Printing Office, February 1996a.

Presidential Advisory Committee on Gulf War Veterans' Illnesses (2002). *Special Report.* Washington D.C: U.S. Government Printing Office

PGVCB. (1997). *Annual Report to Congress: Federally Sponsored Research on Persian Gulf Veterans' Illnesses for 1996.* Washington, DC: VA, 1997.

Quarantelli, E. L. (1998). *Major criteria for judging disaster planning and managing and their applicability in the developing societies.* Disaster Research Center, University of Delaware. Newark, DE.

Report by the National Gulf War Resource Center, Inc. (1996). "Gulf War Syndrome." Fall 1996, p. 5 (in subcommittee files). Washington, DC.

Rostker, B. (1998). Environmental Exposure Report: Depleted Uranium in the Gulf. U. S. Department of Defense Special Assistant for Gulf War Illness, July 31, 1998, p. 4, Sec. 2.

Rostker B. (1997). Vets' health comes first. *USA Today,* July 29, 1997.

Samet, J.M., Dominici, F., Curriero F.C., Coursac, I., & Zeger, S.L. (2000). Fine particulate air pollution and mortality in 20 U.S. cities, 1987-1994. *New England Journal of Medicine* 343(24): 1742-1749.

The Human & Environmental cost of Wars

Schröder, H., Heimers, A., Frentzel-Beyme R., Schott, A., & Hoffmann, W. (2003). Chromosome aberration analysis in peripheral lymphocytes of Gulf War and Balkans War veterans. *Radiation Protection Dosimetry,* 2003, 103:211-220.

Schwartz, J., Norris. G., Larson. T., Sheppard. L., Claiborne, C., & Koenig, J. (1996**).** Episodes of High Coarse Particle Concentrations Are Not Associated with Increased Mortality. *Environmental Health Perspectives* Vol.107, No. 5, May 1999.

Sharp, G., Mizuno, T., Cologne, J. B, Fukuhara, T., Fujiwara, S., Tokuoka, S., et al. (2002). Hapatocellular carcinoma among atomic bomb survivors: significant interaction of radiation with hepatitis C virus infections. *International Journal of Cancer* 103:531-7.

Simon, T. R., Hickey, D.C., Fincher, C.E., Johnson, A.R., Ross, G.H., & Rea, W.J. (1994). Single photon emission computed tomography of the brain in patients with chemical sensitivities. *Toxicology and Industrial Health,* 1994, 10 (4-5):573-577.

Skorga, P, Persell, D. J, Gilbert-Palmrer, Winters, R. Stokes E. N, et al. (2003). Caring for victims of nuclear and radiological terrorism. *Nurse Practitioner,* 28:24-41.

Steele, L. (2000). Prevalence and pattern of Gulf war illnesses in Kansas veterans: association of symptoms with characteristics of persons, place, and time of military service. *American Journal of Epidemiology*, 2000, 152, 992-1002.

Ibid idem 2001, 154:406-407

Strauss, A., & Corbin, J. (1990). *Basics of Qualitative Research: Grounded Theory, Procedures and Techniques.* Newbury Park, CA: Sage Publication.

Stretch, R., Bliese, P., Marlowe, D., Wright, K., Knudson, K., & Hoover, C. (1995). Physical health symptomatology of gulf war era service personnel from the states of Pennsylvania and Hawaii. *Military Medicine*, 160, 131-136.

Skorga P., Persell, D. J., Gilbert-Palmrer., Winters, R., Stokes E. N, et al., (2003). Caring for victims of nuclear and radiological terrorism. *Nurse Practitioner* 28:24-41.

Senate Veterans' Affairs Committee (1998). *Report of the Special Investigation Unit on Gulf War Illnesses.* Washington DC: U.S. Government Printing Office.

The Human & Environmental cost of Wars

Serrano, R. (1994) *Los Angeles Times* Nov. 14, 1994.

Taylor, S. J., & Bogden, R. (1984). *Introduction to Qualitative Research Methods: The Search for Meaning.* (2nd ed). New York: John Wiley and Sons.

Taylor, S. J., & Bogden, R. (1998). *"Working with Data," Introduction to Qualitative Research Methods* (Third Edition). New York: John Wiley and Sons.

Time Magazine, Jan 09, 2001

Time Magazine, Jan 25, 2003

Twigg, John. (2002). *NGO Initiatives in Risk Reduction: An Annotated Bibliography of case studies.* Version 1, March 2002, London: University College London, Gower Street.

Unwin C., Blatchley, N., & Coker, W., et al. (1999). Health of U.K. Serviceman Who Served in the Persian Gulf War. *The Lancet*, 353:169-178.

U.S. Congress, Committee on Government Reform and Oversight, Gulf War Veterans Illnesses: VA, DOD Continue to Resist Strong Evidence Linking Toxic Causes to Chronic Health Effects, (November 7, 1997).

USACHPPM. (2000). *Depleted Uranium in the Gulf.* Office of Special Assistant to the Sec, of Def, for Gulf War Illnesses, Medical Readiness and Military Deployments. (OSAGW), HRA Consultation no. 26-MF-7555-000, September 15, 2000.

U.S. Nuclear Regulatory Commission. (1999). *Systemic Radiological Assessment of Exemptions for Source and Byproduct Materials.* Draft Report, Uranium in Counterweights, Washington, DC, December 1999.

White, G.F. (1974). *Natural Hazards, Local, National, Global.* New York: Oxford University Press.

World Health Organization Report. (2001). *Depleted Uranium Sources, Exposure and Health Effects.* April 2001.

World Health Organization (2002). *Environmental Health Information. Depleted Uranium: sources, exposure and health effects.* Geneva, WHO/SDE/PHE/01.1.

United Nations Report by the Secretary-General Submitted Pursuant to Sub-Commission Resolution 1996/16. *Commission on Human Rights, Sub-Commission on Prevention of Discrimination and Protection of Minorities.* Forty-ninth session, Geneva Switzerland, June 24, 1997, p. 2.

UNEP. (2000). Meeting Minutes. *Balkans Task Force Expert Group Meeting on Potential Effects on Human Health and the Environment Arising from the Use of Depleted Uranium During the 1999 Kosovo Conflict.* Geneva, Switzerland. March, 20, 2000.

UNEP. (2000) *NATO confirms to the UN use of depleted uranium during the Kosovo conflict.* Press release from the United Nations Environment Programme, Geneva, Switzerland. March 21, 2000.
http://www.grid.unep.ch/btf/pressreleases/unep21032000.html

US Army Environmental Policy Institute (1995) *Health and Environmental Consequences of Depleted Uranium Use in the US Army: Technical Report*, Atlanta, GA: Georgia Institute of Technology.

U.S. News and World Report. July 8, 1996.

Younger, S. M. (2000). *Nuclear Weapons in the Twenty-first Century, Los Alamos National Laboratory*, LAUR-00-2850, June 27, p. 13-15.

Znaniecki, F. (1934). *The Method of Sociology.*
New York, Rinehard. Co. Inc.

The Human & Environmental cost of Wars

The Human & Environmental cost of Wars

The Human & Environmental cost of Wars

The Human & Environmental cost of Wars

The Human & Environmental cost of Wars

The Human & Environmental cost of Wars